The golden moments in the stream of life rush past us and we see nothing but sand; the angels come to visit us, and we only know them when they are gone.
George Eliot

I momenti d'oro, nel torrente della vita, scorrono cosi veloci davanti a noi, che non ci è dato di vedere nient'altro che la sabbia. Gli angeli ci fanno visita e noi ce ne accorgiamo soltanto quando sono partiti per sempre.

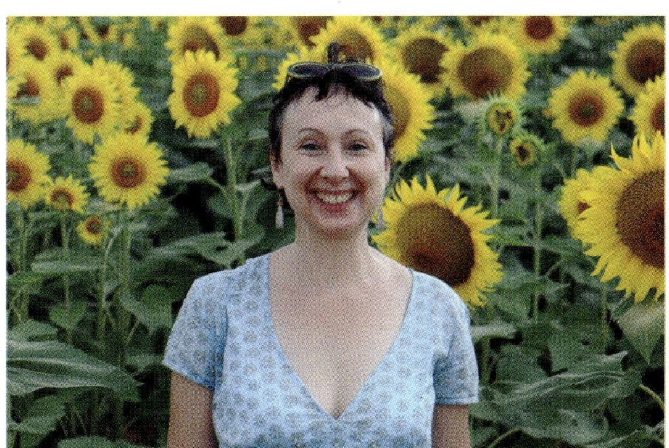

Anita Klein

Anita Klein • Italian Angels

Anita Klein Italian Angels
Five Leaves Publications 2009, PO Box 8786, Nottingham NG1 9AW
www.fiveleaves.co.uk
www.anitaklein.com

Photography Nigel Swift
Design Rivierakid
www.rivierakid.com
Printed in London by Aduo Colour Ltd.

Grazie alle mie amiche:
Mara Benetti, Elisa Giudice e
Lucia Demaria per la traduzione

Five Leaves is pleased to acknowledge support from Arts Council England.

ISBN: 978 1 905512 59 1

In the summer of 2006 we went on a family holiday to Tuscany. While we were there, two exciting things happened. Italy won the world cup. And my mum bought a flat in a small town called Anghiari, on the border of Tuscany and Umbria. "What does signing mean?" she asked naïvely as she remortgaged our house in London, but there was no way anyone could convince her to change her mind. She had fallen in love with the flat, and with it, she had fallen in love with Anghiari.

Two and a half years later, and we are all beginning to understand why she felt so strongly. It's not just that the flat, with its airy, square rooms and marble floors is beautifully peaceful, but also that Anghiari is almost the antithesis of South East London, where we've lived as a family all of my life. Anghiari's streets and buildings are neatly rounded on the side of a hill, almost as if someone had built the town out of sand and patted its sides till they were smooth. Its inhabitants are gentle, friendly people whose families have lived in the region for generations, and who stop in the streets to talk to each other whatever else they might have been doing. And, perhaps most differently to South London, Anghiari is a town whose history is very much a part of its present.

From the sombre masked march up the main street at Easter, to the Palio in June in which the town's inhabitants re-enact the ancient battle of Anghiari, the town is alive with traditions. Some of them, like these, have probably existed for hundreds, if not thousands, of years. But there are other, smaller traditions which seem to shape everyday life – traditions which most of us wouldn't think twice about. Every day you know when the fish seller will arrive, or when the church bells are going to ring, when the shops are going to shut mid-afternoon, and even when the next-door neighbours will hang out their washing. There is, surprisingly enough for Italy, a general lack of chaos.

My mum's work has always been a celebration of the things we repeat over and over again in our lives – a cup of tea in the afternoon, chopping an onion, watching EastEnders – so for her, seeing these traditions confirmed everything her work rejoices in. Being in Anghiari for one week a month (a routine she now firmly sticks to) has given her the chance to create her own traditions and to notice the broader patterns in life which she otherwise doesn't have time to spot. And, because she is there at so many different points over the year, she has enough distance to notice the tiny transformations which locals are probably immune to.

With the changing seasons come new festivals and traditions in the town, but also new flowers in the fields, different weather, and new fruit in the shops. And with each new season, my mum's own daily routine changes, too. In the winter she paints all morning and goes for a walk through the fields in the afternoon. In the summer, she paints all day and only ventures out when it is cool enough in the evening. She has become a seamless part of the town, fitting in to the artistic tradition of the region (Anghiari is surrounded by Piero della Francesca's frescoes), learning Italian well enough to make friends with the locals, and even being invited to two weddings in Anghiari's medieval church.

I suppose it's now quite obvious where the angels came from. But without this explanation, it would be easy for people, particularly fans of my mum's work, to question how the series fits with her past pictures of our family. What do ploughed fields have in common with a family having breakfast? How is autumn in any way related to a surprise birthday cake? The answer, which I hope most people will have realised after reading my description of Anghiari, is that they are all small things which people have been doing for thousands of years. Each one of the 52 angels is a celebration of something which most people overlook, or wouldn't think twice about. They are not celebrations of success, careers or material things (although Angel of the Boots might be an exception!), but fleeting moments in time which have been captured and squeezed into frames. In Anghiari, a place where all these cycles, patterns and routines fit so perfectly together, it seems only right that there is some kind of spiritual force watching over each one, making sure it fits with the rest.

Some angels, like the Angel of the Snow and the Angel of the Rain, are huge, towering over mountains and watching over whole towns. Others, like the Angel of the Strawberries (my favourite) are tiny, hiding cheekily under leaves or sitting amongst the flowers. But all of them, whatever they represent, have been drawn on paper of the same size and dimensions, and have been painted with acrylic – a departure from my mum's usual choice of oil paints (it's not easy to transport boards between Italy and England). So the Angel of the Palio fills the same size frame as the Angel of the Laundry, and the Angel of Spring matches the Angel of the Mosquito bite. There is no discrimination between big events and small ones, and no division between specific images, like the white cat who lives in the flat below, and more general ones, like the mist which envelops Anghiari on autumn mornings.

A lot of the paintings have personal stories behind them, like the Angel of the Christmas Lights who is wrapped in a blanket because my mum once went to the flat in December and had to stay under a duvet until the heating kicked in. Or the Angel Surprised by a Pheasant, who was inspired by a walk on an autumn day through the local fields. But for most people, these stories are irrelevant. The angels, like the everyday pictures of our family, are recognised by almost every person who looks at them. Everyone knows how soft a peach is, or how relieving a gentle breeze can be on a stiflingly hot day. These pictures make us conscious of these moments – they make us stop and think about how each one feels, or about what each one means.

My mum once said that to judge if a picture is any good, she imagines it as a fresco on the wall of a church. If she thinks it would make people smile, then it's good enough. What's amazing about this series of paintings is that each one would make someone smile whether they were from the year 1200, or the year 3000. They are not of fashions or fads, or things we will look back on and cringe over. They are of things that people have always enjoyed and will always relate to. And for that, they are timeless.

Maia Swift 2009

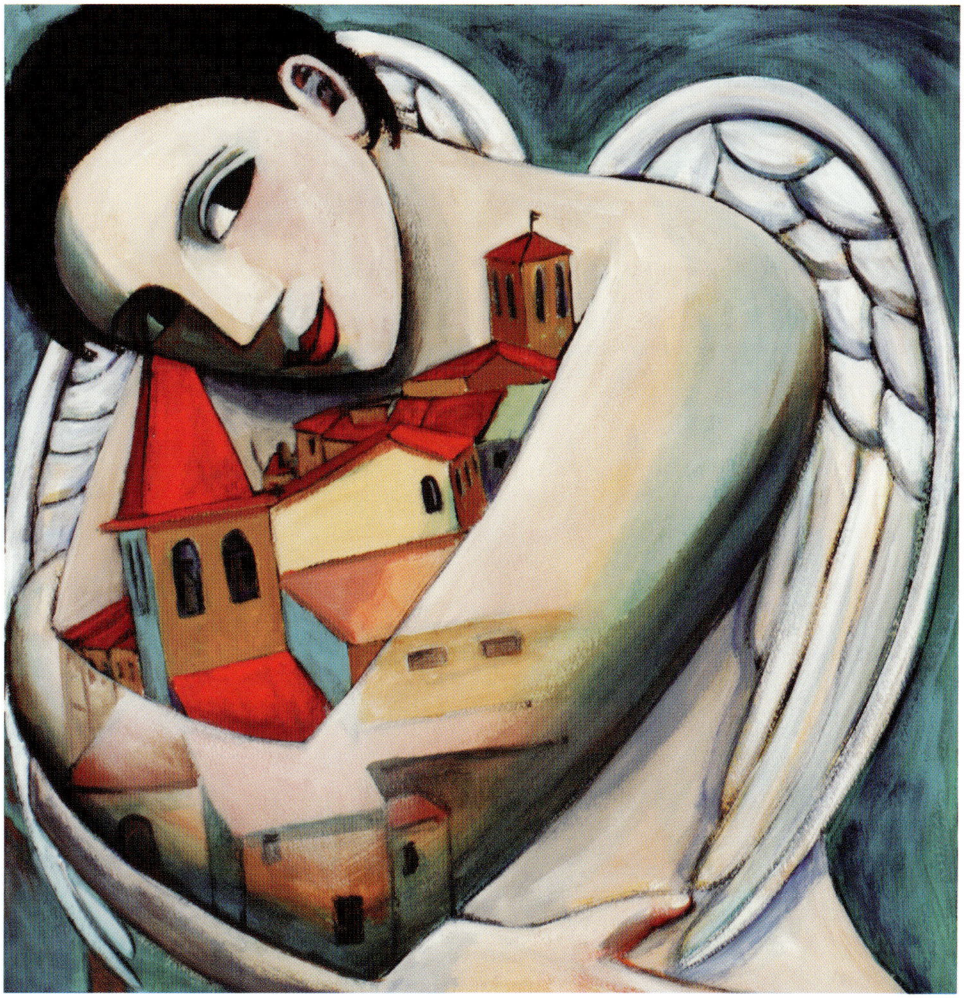

Angelo della Nebbia

The healthy air of morning fell like breath from angels, on the sleeping town.
Charles Dickens - The Old Curiosity Shop

L'aria salubre del mattino scende come un respiro, dagli angeli, sulla città addormentata.

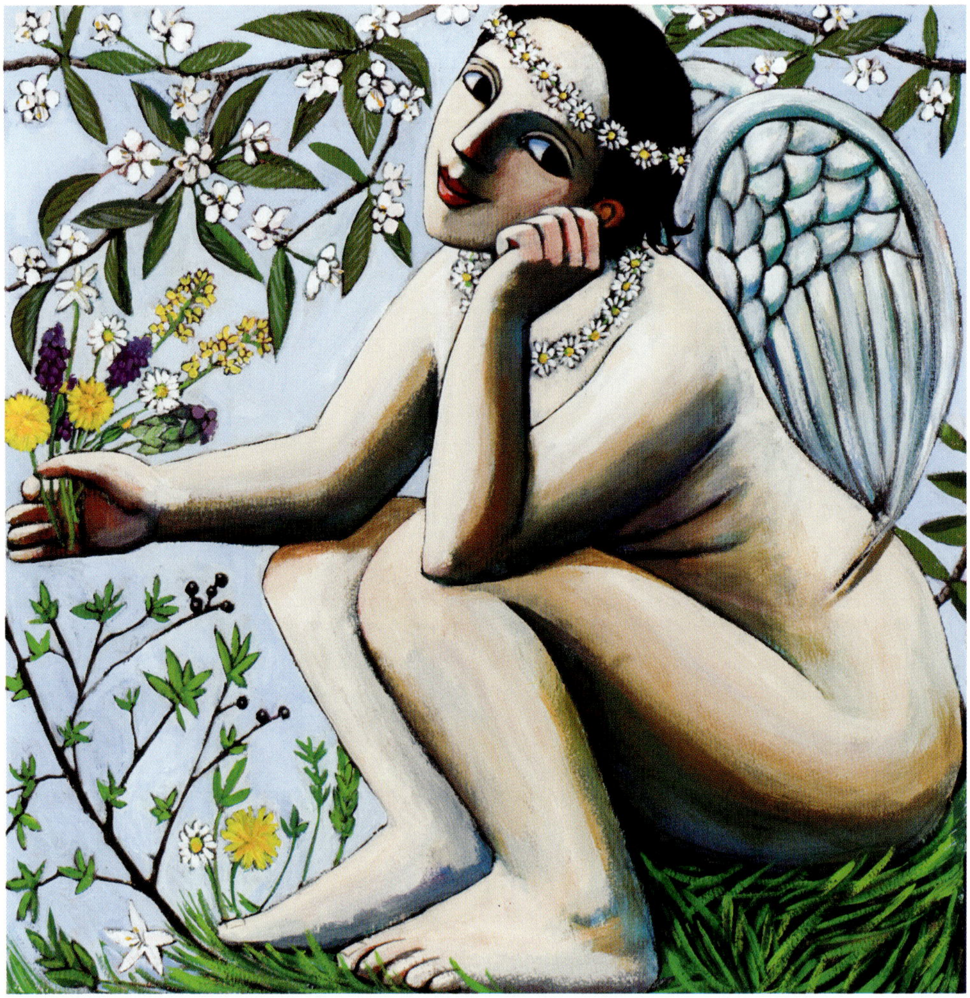

Angelo della Primavera

Silently, one by one, in the infinite meadows of heaven,
Blossomed the lovely stars, the forget-me-nots of the angels.
Henry Wadsworth Longfellow - Evangeline

Silenziose, l'una dopo l'altra, nei pascoli infiniti del paradiso
Sono fiorite stelle bellissime, i nontiscordardimè degli angeli.

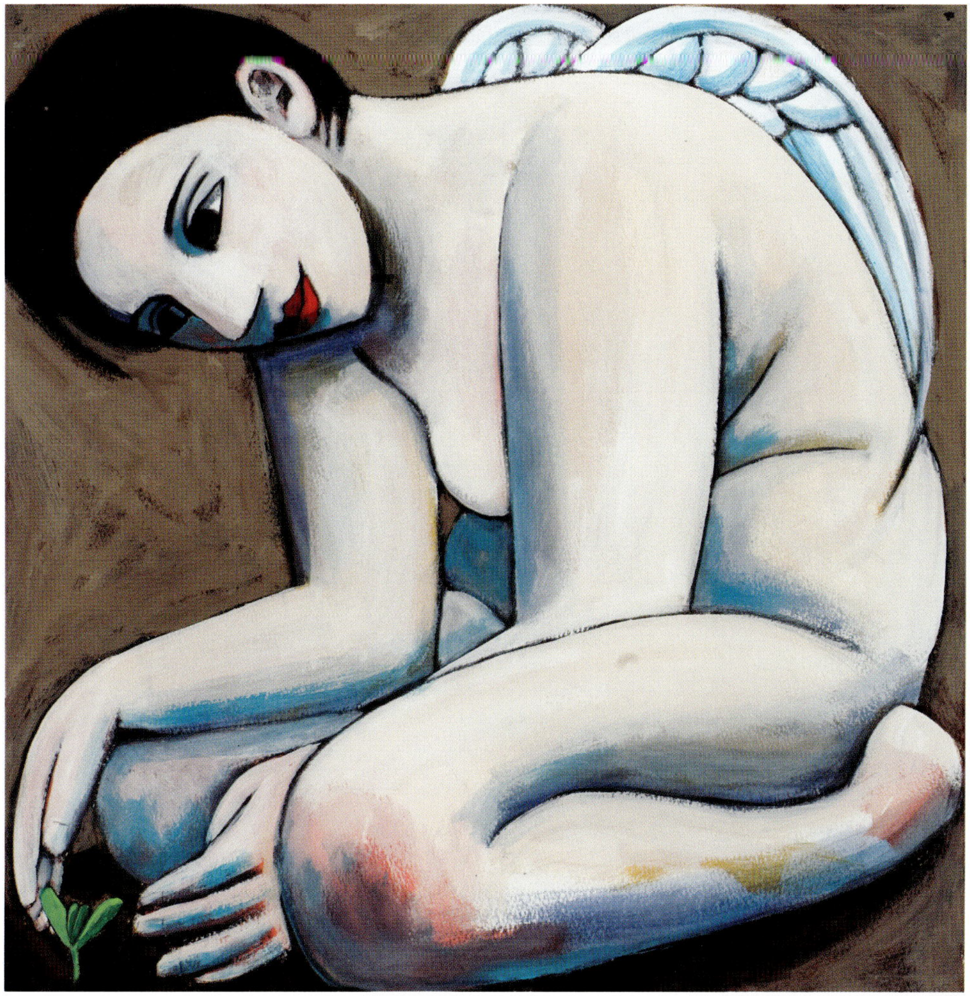

Angelo della Piantina

Every blade of grass has an angel that bends over it and whispers "grow! grow!" *The Talmud*

Ogni filo d'erba ha un angelo che, curvato sopra di esso, gli sussurra "Cresci! Cresci!"

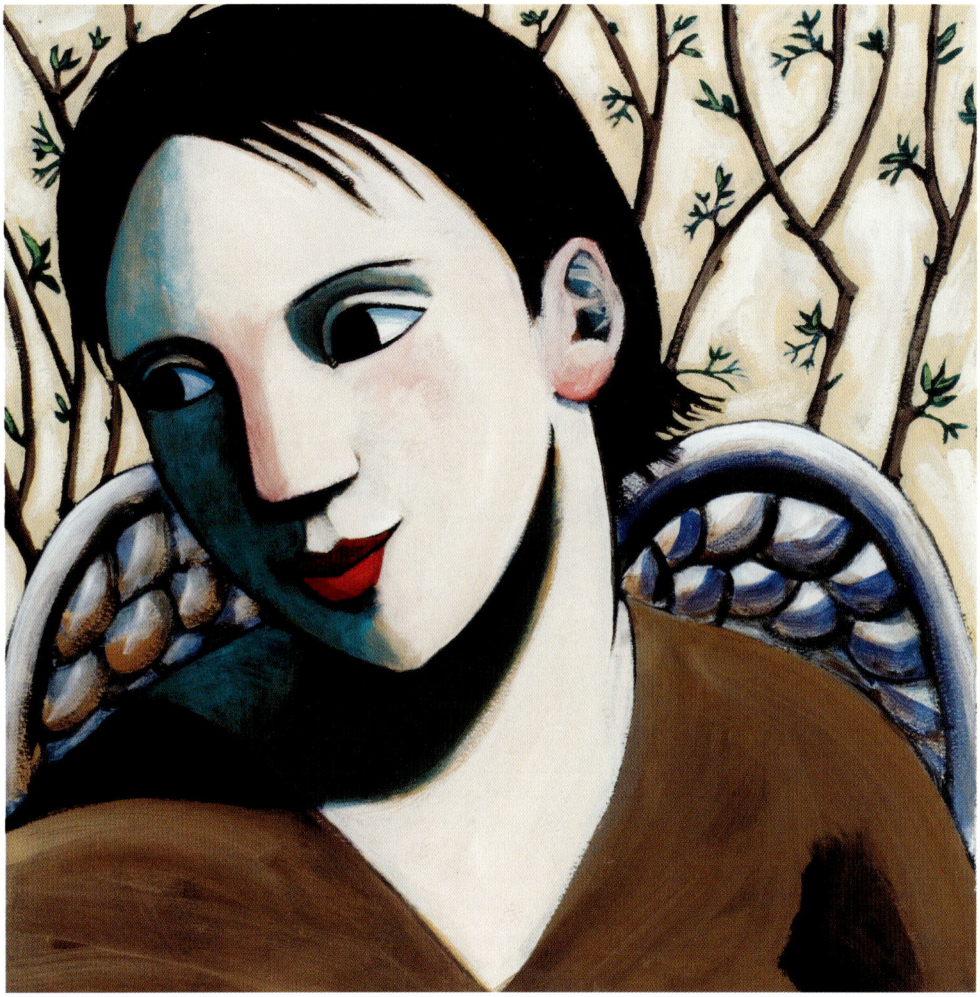

Angelo dei Germogli

Never place a full stop where your angel has placed a comma. *Anonymous*

Non mettere mai un punto dove il tuo angelo ha messo una virgola.

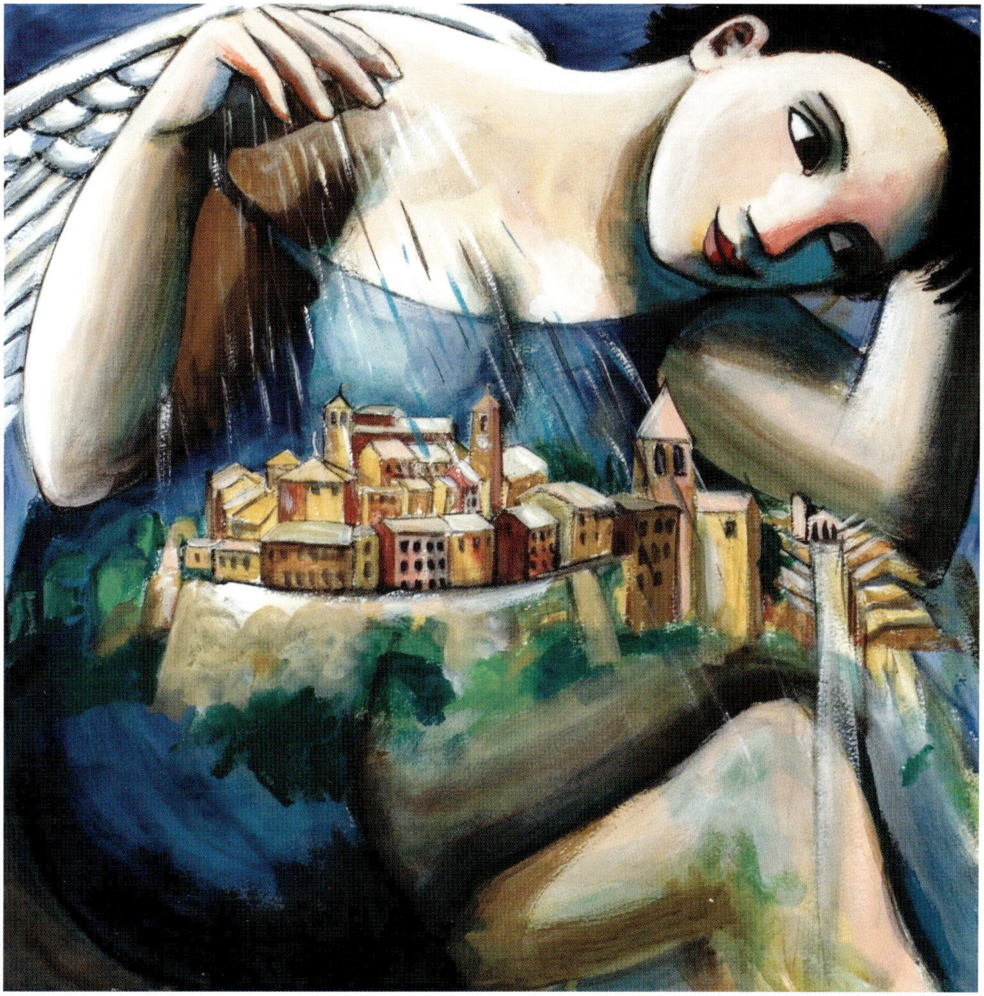

Angelo della Pioggia

“All right,” the angel said, “I will grant your request. I will not destroy that little village...” *Bible - Genisis 19:21*

“Va bene” disse l’angelo, “accoglierò la tua richiesta. Non distruggerò quel piccolo villaggio...”

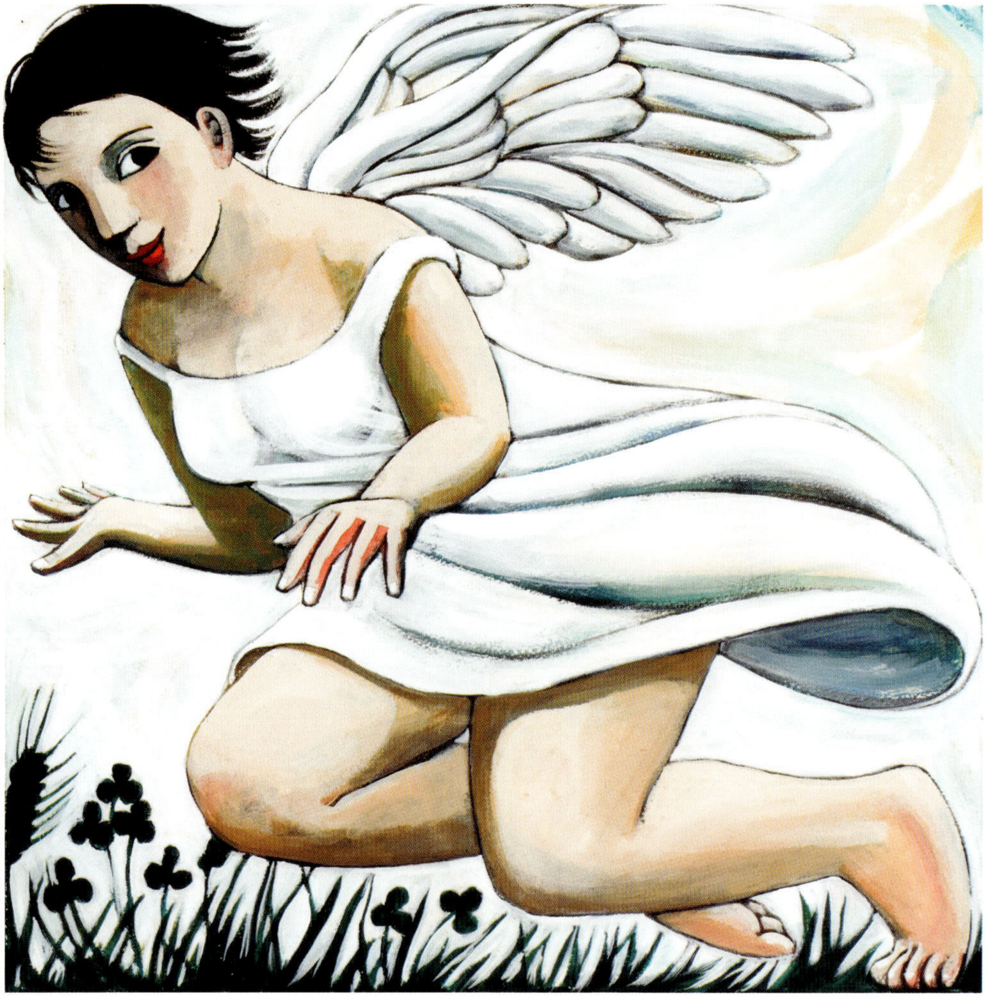

Angelo del Venticello

O welcome, pure-eyed Faith, white-handed Hope,
Thou hovering angel, girt with golden wings! *John Milton - Comus*

Benvenuto, Fede dagli occhi puri, Speranza dalle bianche mani,
Tu, angelo sospeso in volo, adornato di sontuose ali dorate!

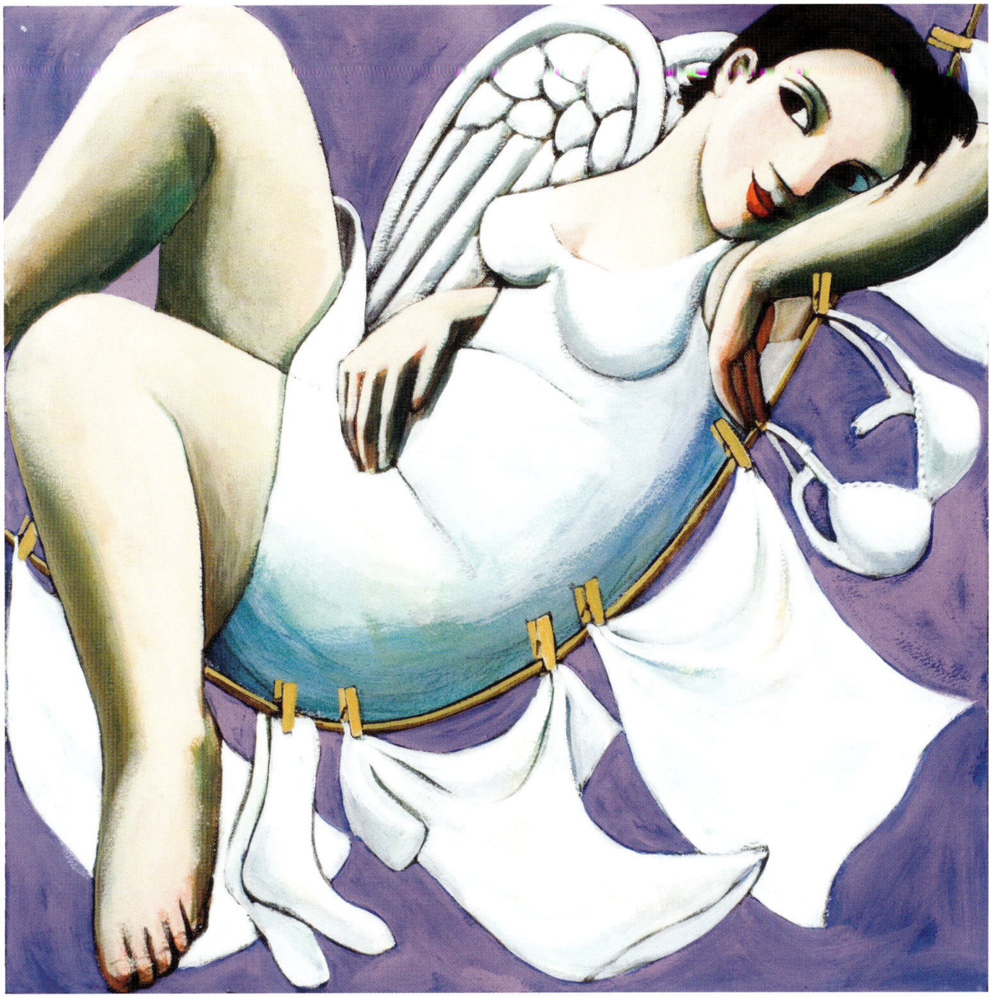

Angelo del Bucato

The guardian angels of life fly so high as to be beyond our sight, but they are always looking down upon us. *Jean Paul Richter*

Gli angeli custodi della vita volano così alti da essere al di sopra della nostra vista, ma ci osservano sempre dall'alto.

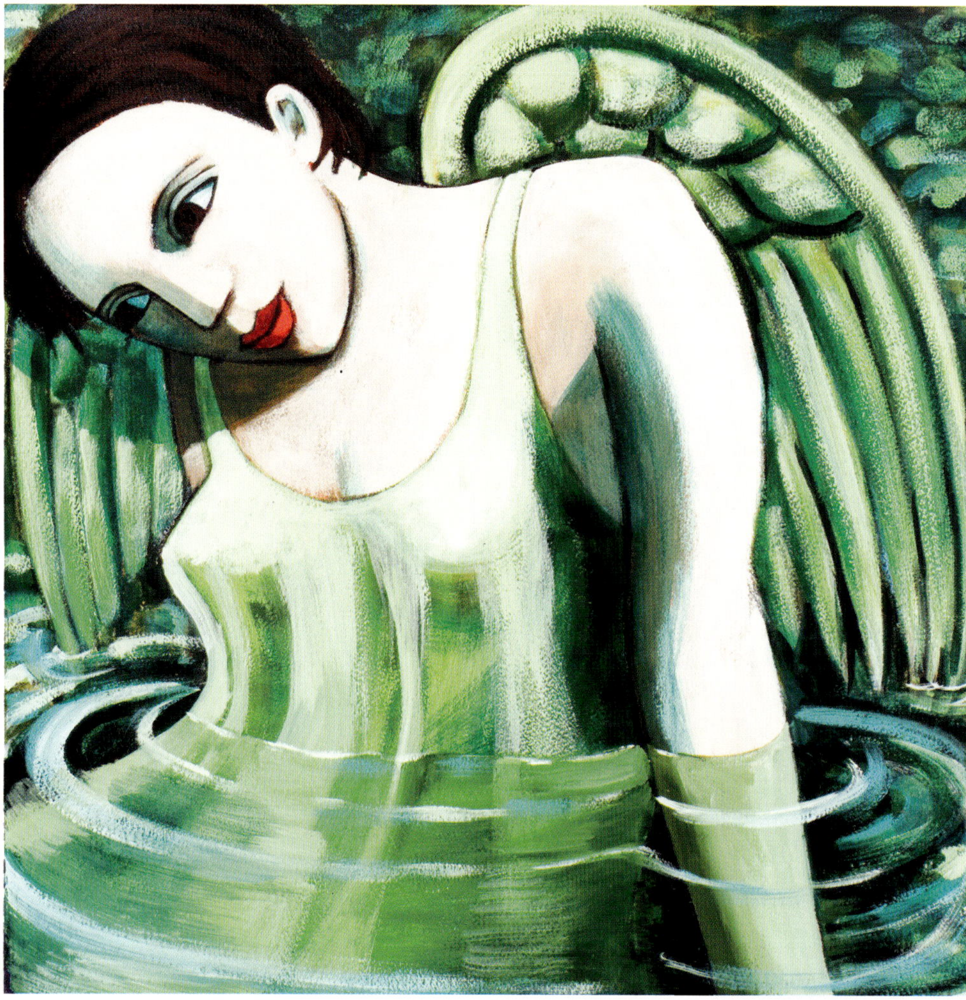

Angelo del Fiume

If trouble hearing Angels song with thine ears, try listening with thy heart.
Meriel Stelliger

Se ti è difficile sentire il canto degli angeli con le orecchie, prova a sentirlo con il cuore.

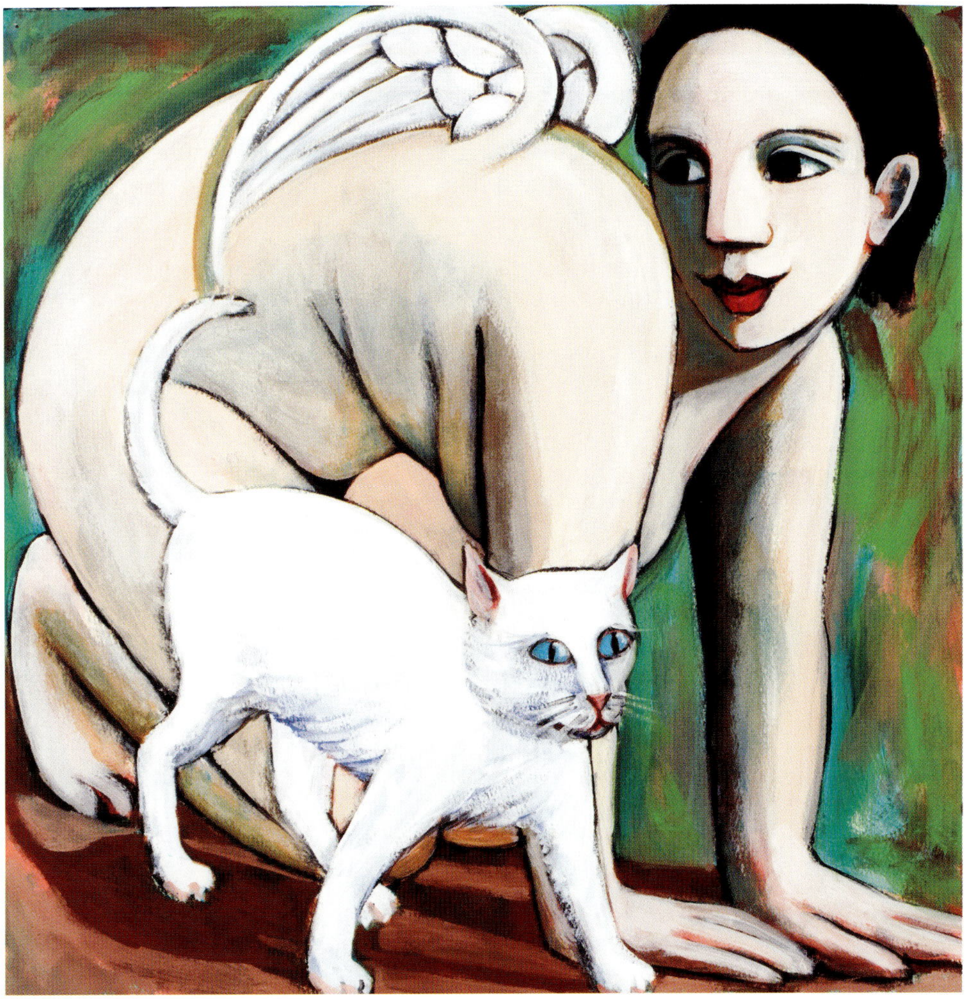

Angelo del Gatto Bianco

See I am sending an angel ahead of you to guard you along the way.
Bible - Exodus 23:20

Ecco, ti mando un angelo perché ti custodisca lungo il cammino.

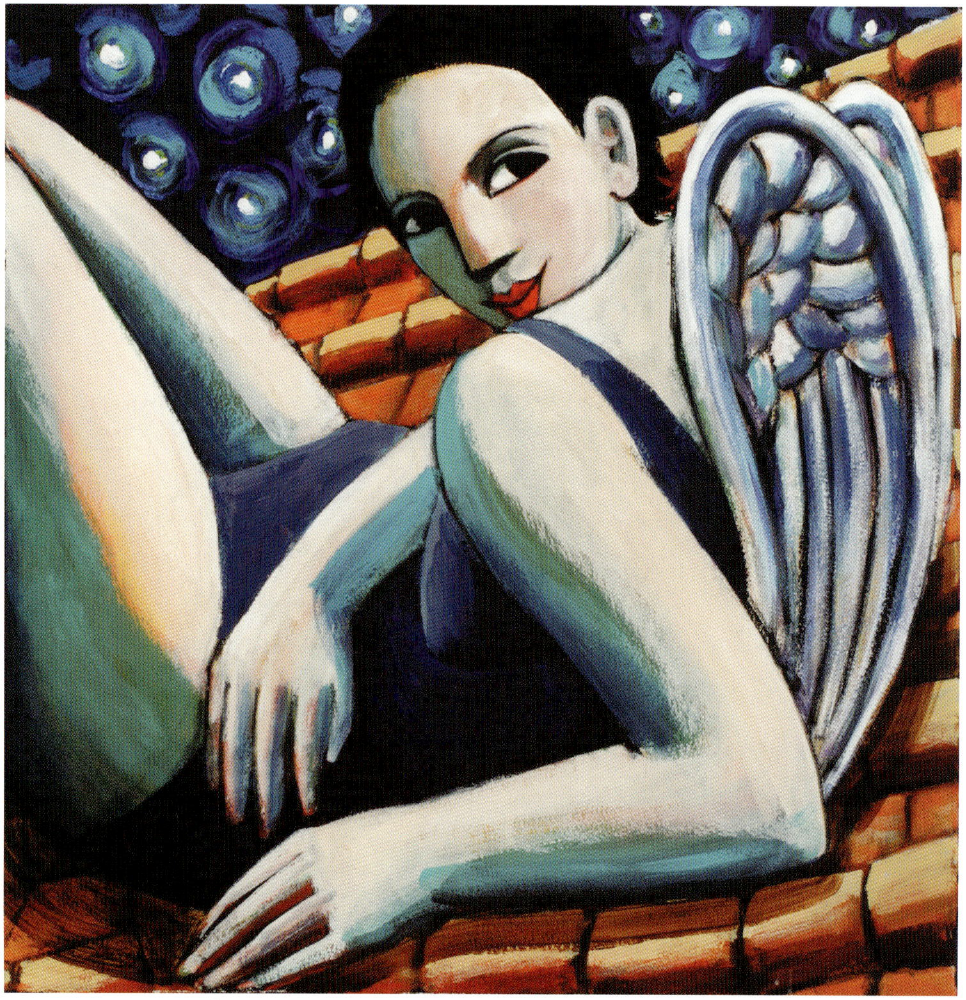

Angelo del Tetto

Every time you hear a bell ring, it means that some angel's just got his wings.
Henry Travers to Jimmy Stewart in It's a Wonderful Life

Quando senti una campana suonare, è perché un angelo ha appena ricevuto un paio d'ali.

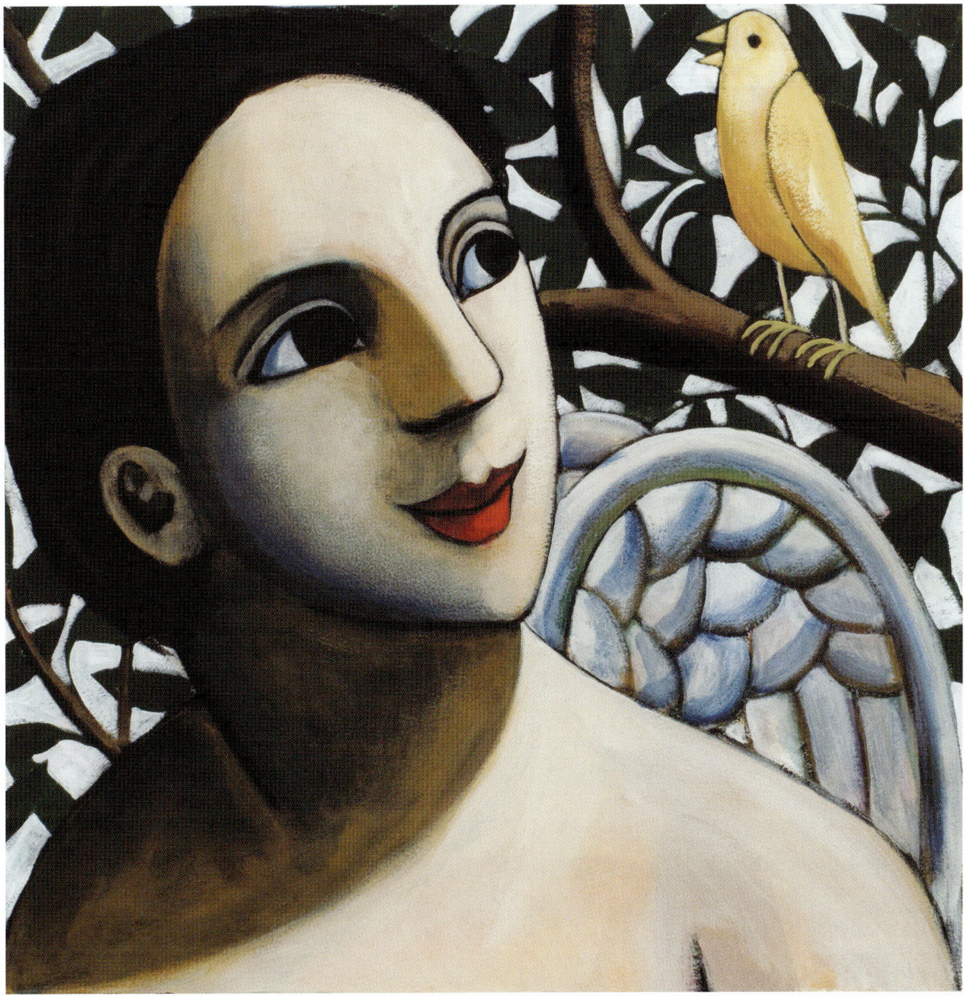

Angelo degli Uccelli

…Sing, creatures, sing,
Angels and men and birds, and everything… *Christina G. Rossetti*

...Cantate, creature, cantate,
angeli, uomini e uccelli, tutti...

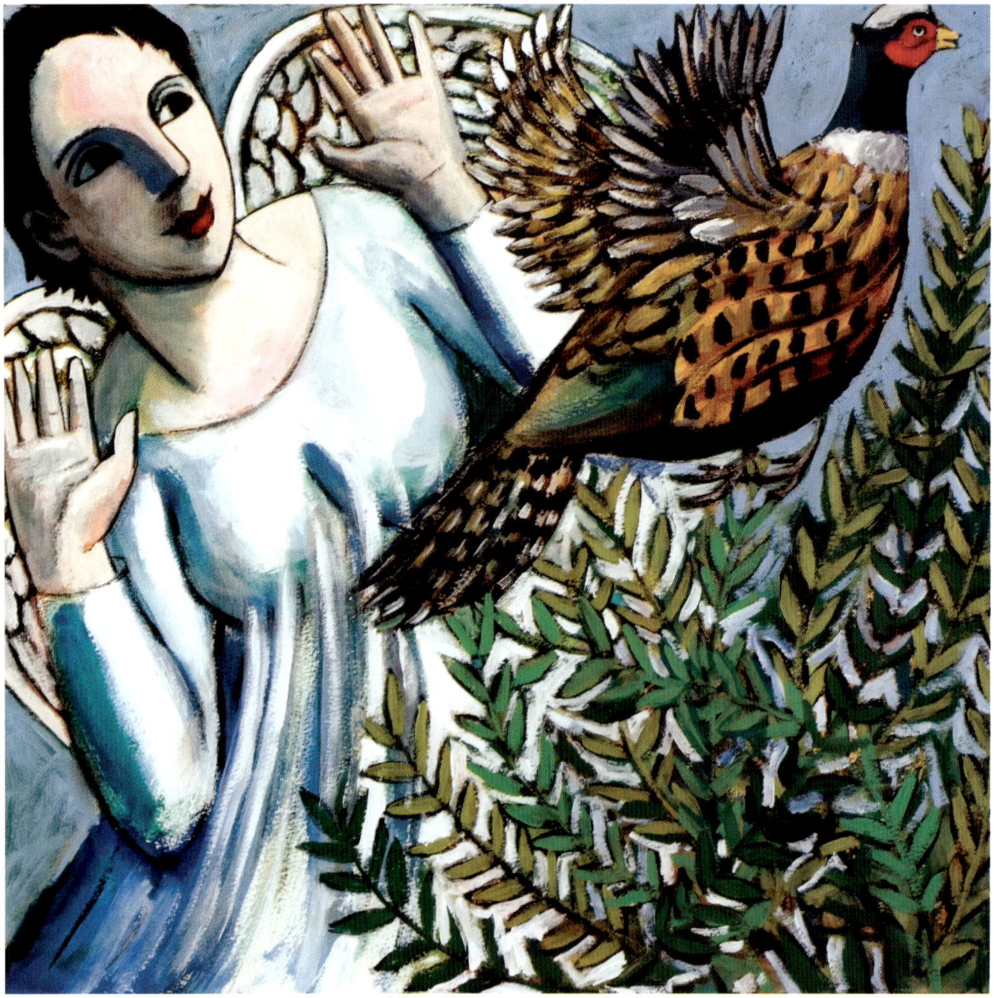

Angelo Sorpreso da un Fagiano

A pillow for thee will I bring,
Stuffed with down of angel's wing. *Richard Crashaw*

Un guanciale per te porterò
Imbottito con piume d'ala di un angelo.

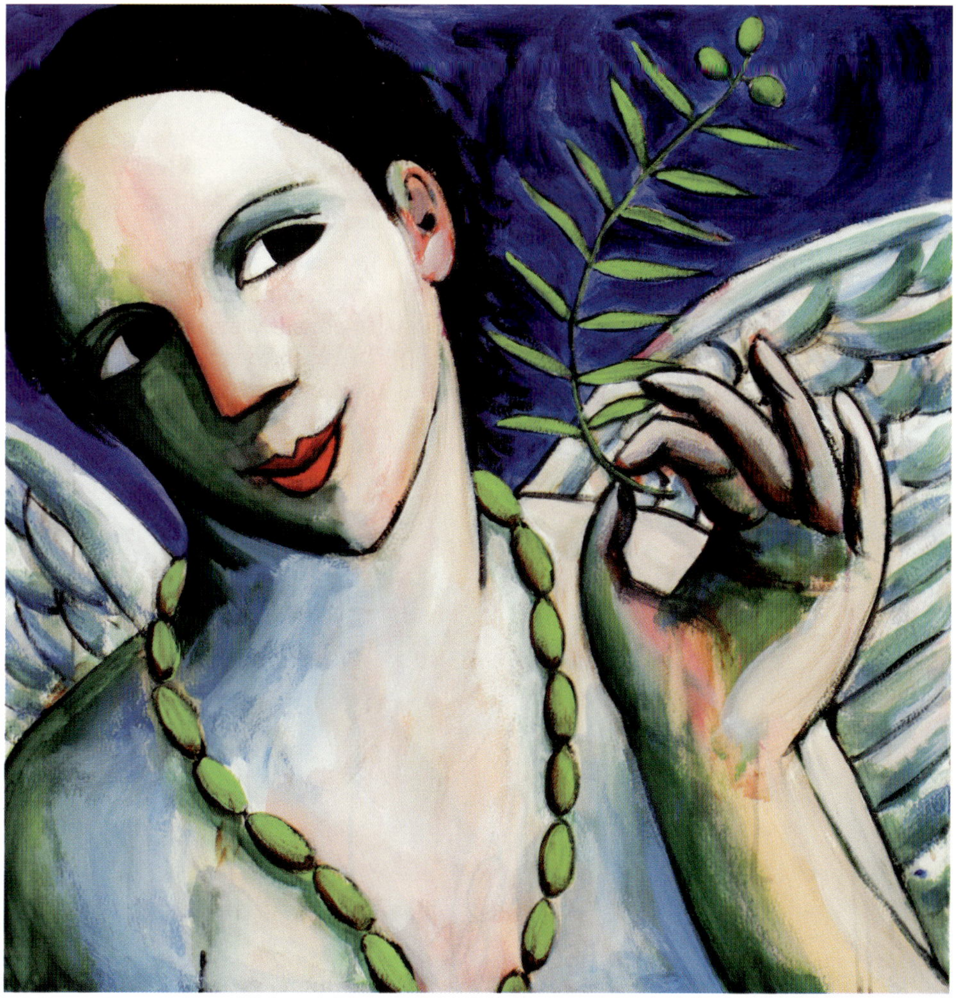

Angelo delle Olive

I wear a coat of angels' breath and warm myself with His love.
Emme Woodhull-Bäche

Indosso un cappotto tessuto con il respiro degli angeli e mi riscaldo con l'amore di Dio.

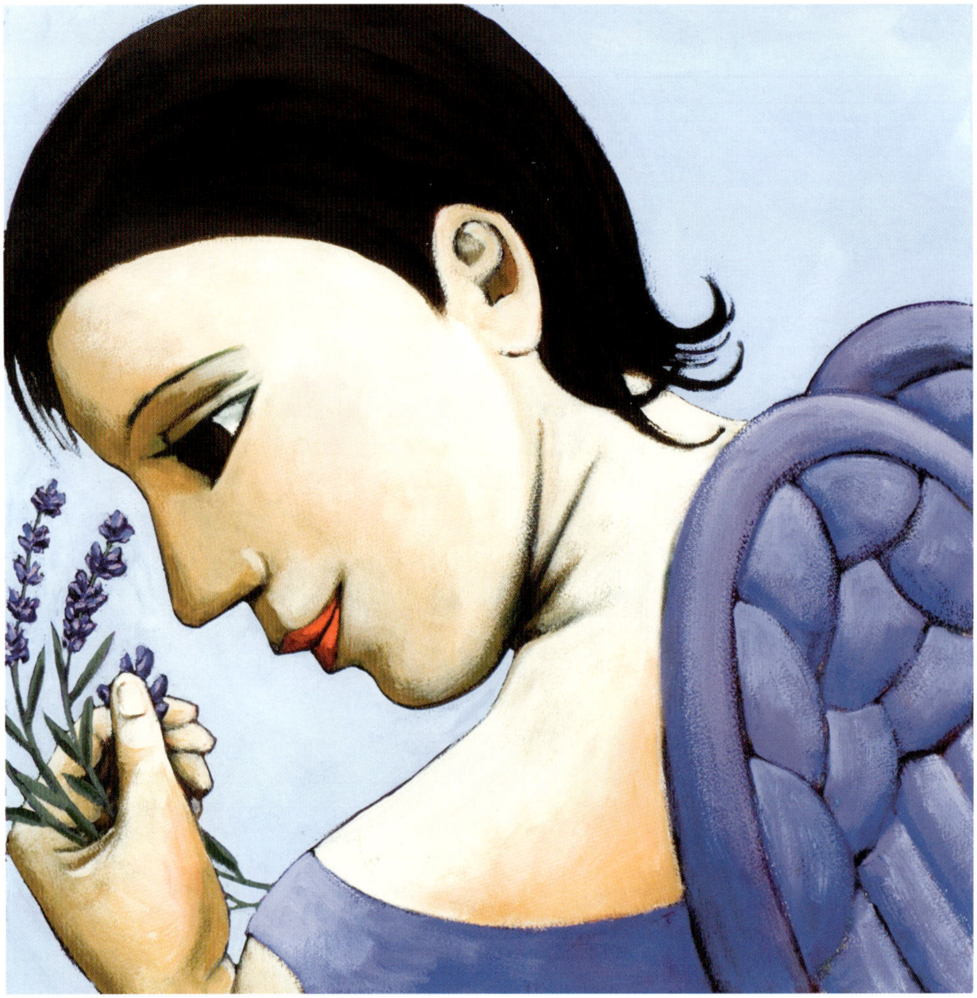

Angelo della Lavanda

If you can't hear the angels, try quieting the static of worry. *Valentine Sterling*

Se non senti gli angeli, prova a calmare i turbamenti dell' ansia.

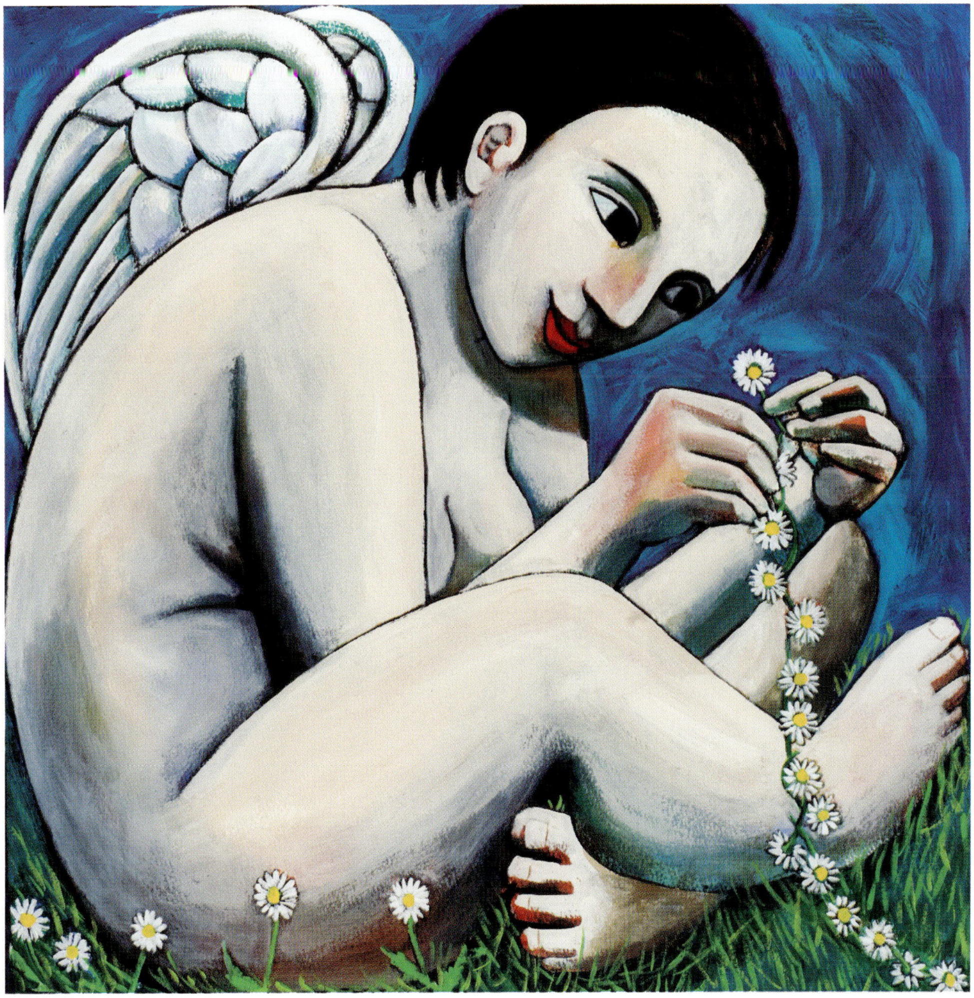

Angelo della Ghirlanda di Margherite

An angel collects all the prayers offered in the synagogues, weaves them into garlands, and puts them on God's head. *Bible - Exodus 21:4*

Un angelo raccoglie tutte le preghiere offerte nelle sinagoghe,
le intreccia nelle ghirlande e le mette sulla testa di Dio.

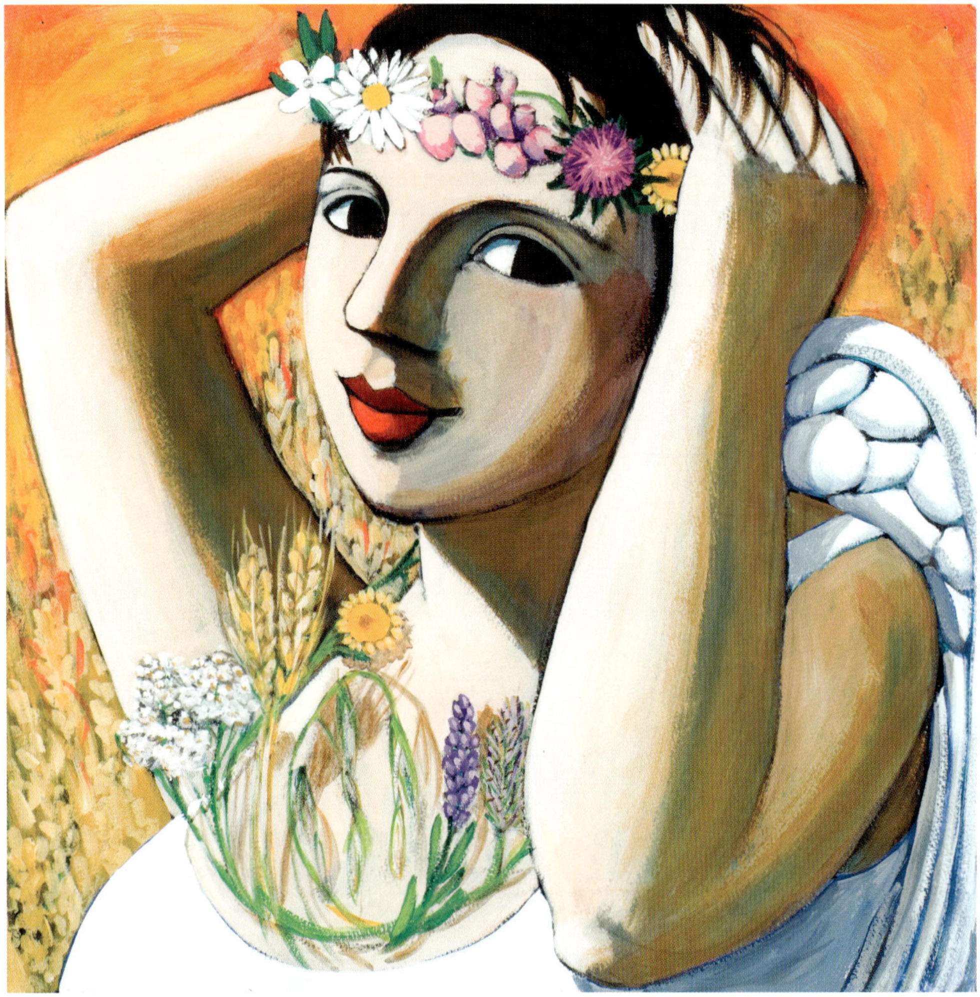

Angelo dell'Estate

Outside the open window
The morning air is all awash with angels. *Richard Purdy Wilbur*

Fuori dalla finestra spalancata
L'aria della mattina è inondata di angeli.

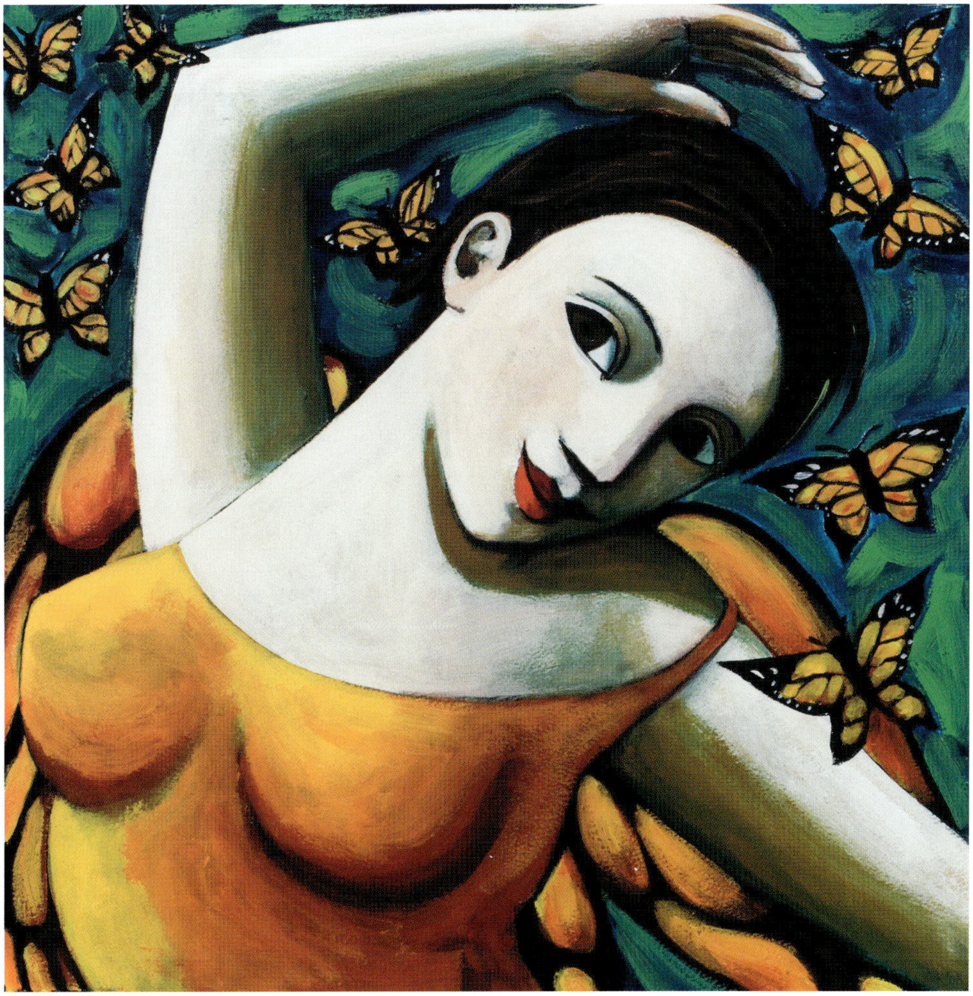

Angelo delle Farfalle

The reason angels can fly is because they take themselves lightly.
G. K. Chesterton - Orthodoxy

Gli angeli possono volare perché vivono nella leggerezza.

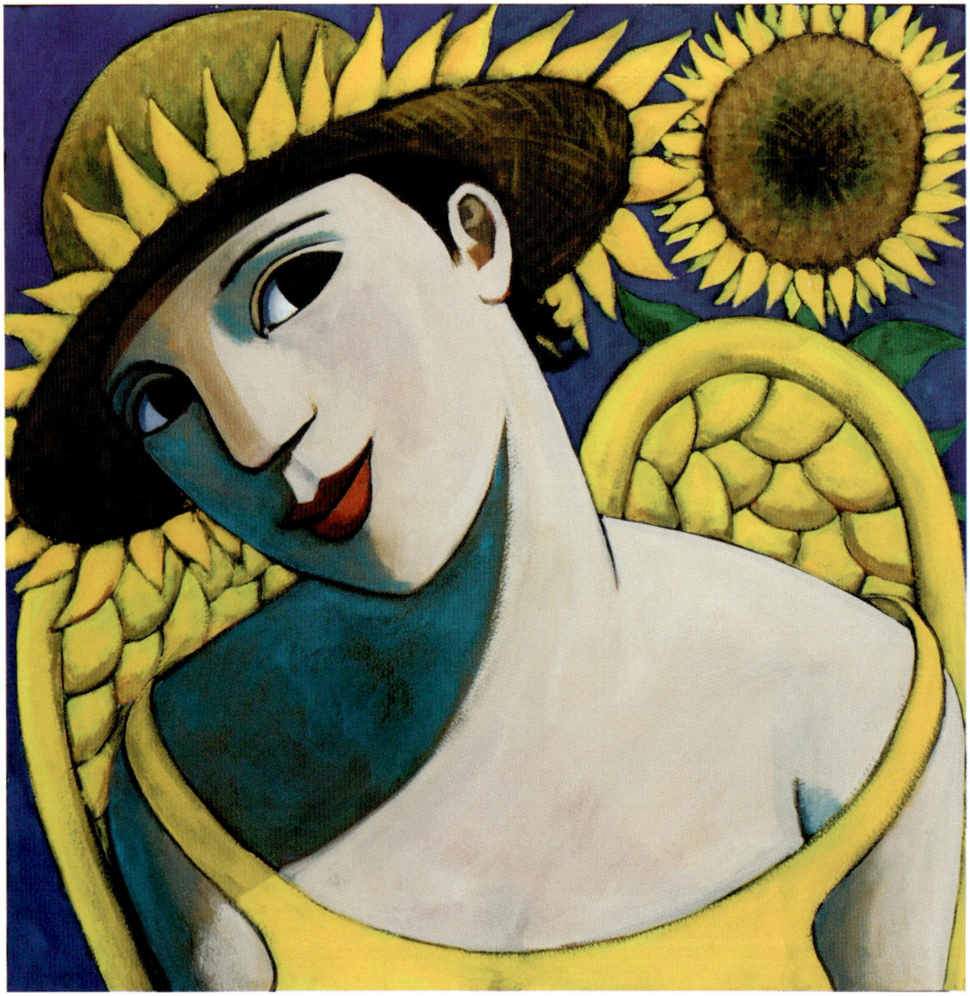

Angelo dei Girasoli

I feel that there is an angel inside me whom I am constantly shocking.
Jean Cocteau

Sento che c'è un angelo dentro di me, che io scandalizzo continuamente.

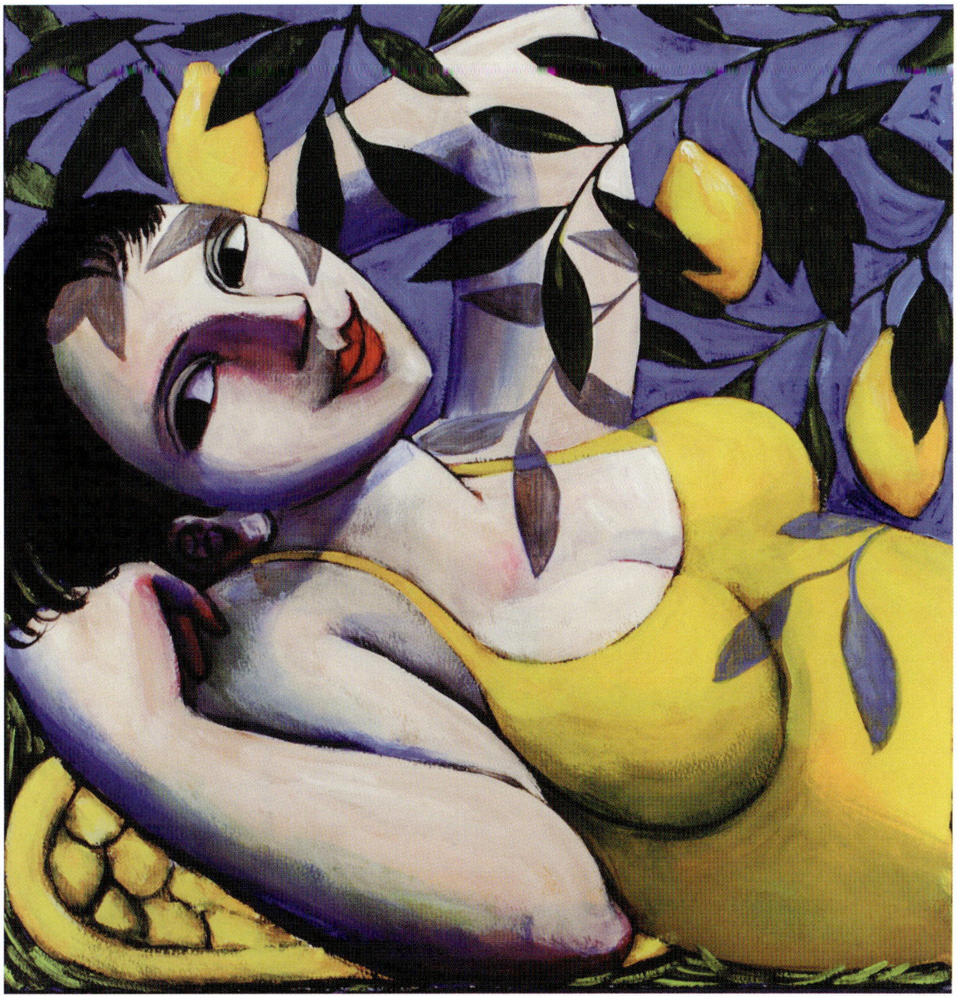

Angelo dei Limoni

I saw the angel in the marble and carved until I set him free. *Michelangelo*

Vidi l’angelo nel marmo e scolpii fino a liberarlo.

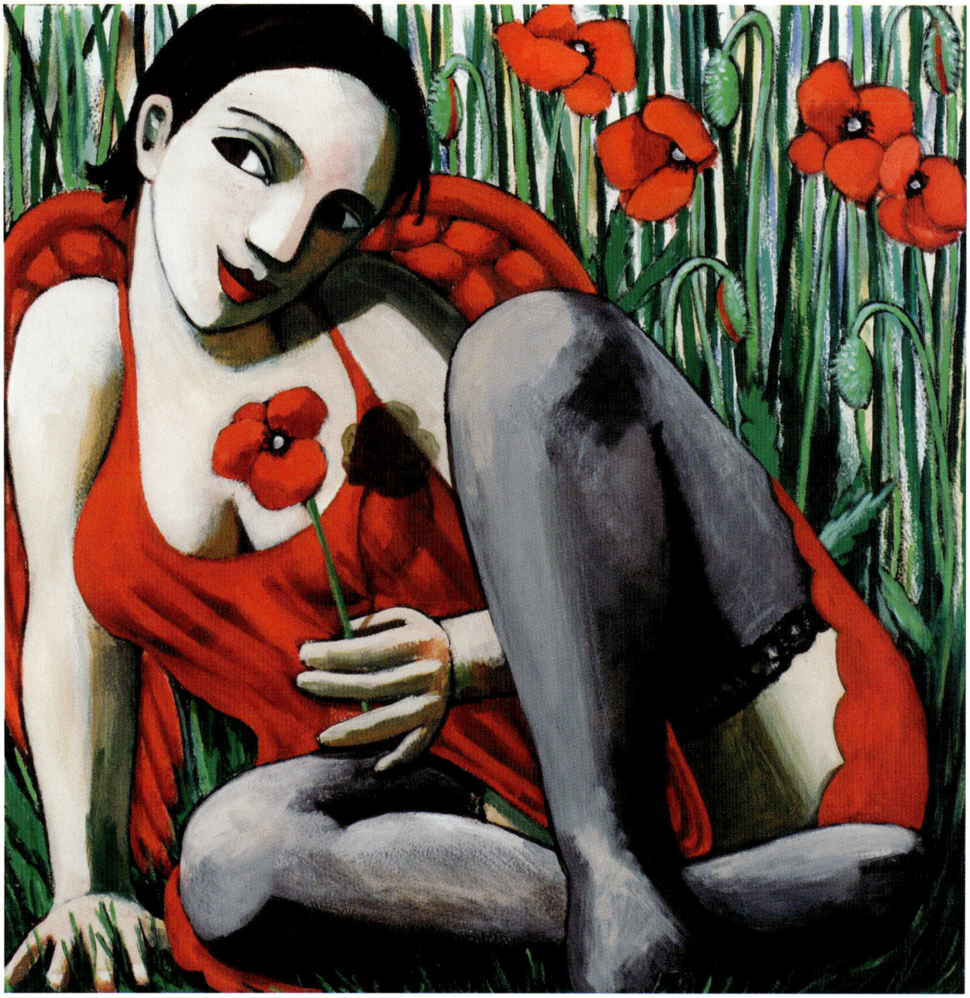

Angelo dei Papaveri

The devil is an angel too. *Miguel de Unamuno*

Anche il diavolo è un angelo.

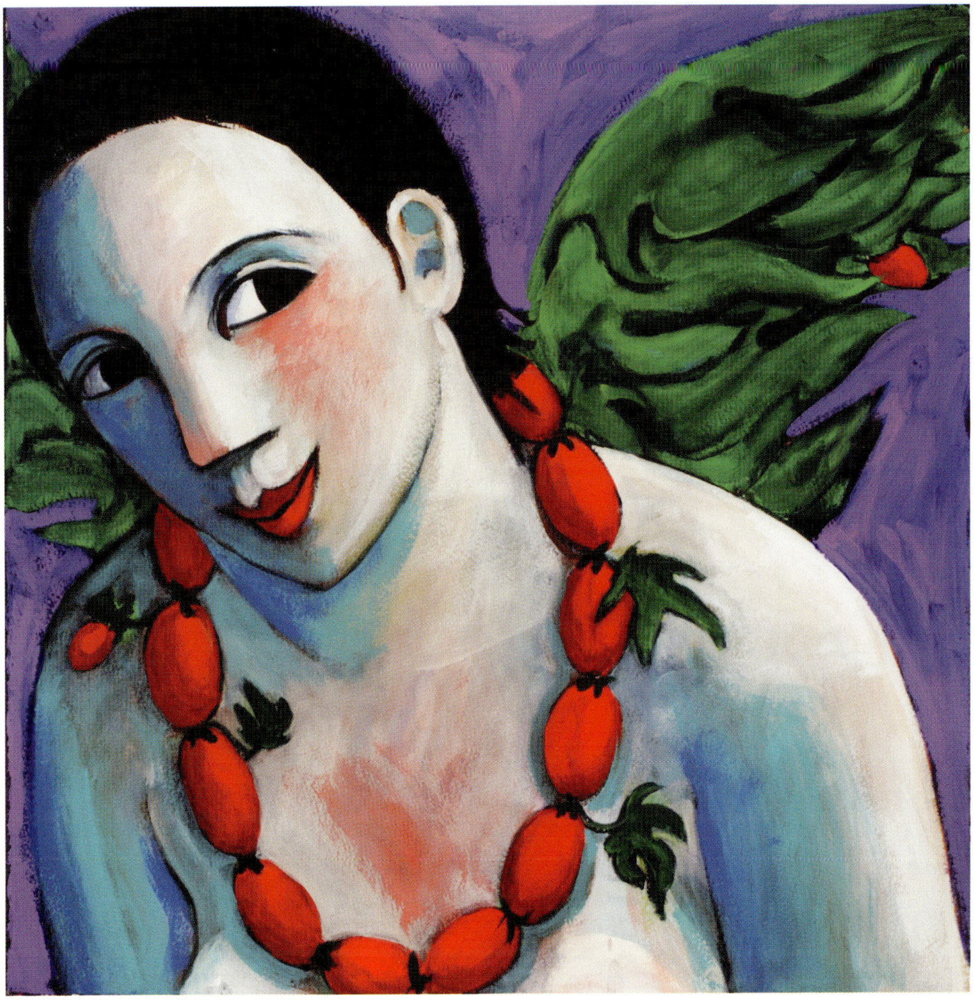

Angelo dei Pomodori

Millions of spiritual creatures walk the earth
Unseen, both when we wake and when we sleep.
John Milton - Paradise Lost

Milioni di creature spirituali si muovono, non viste, sulla terra, quando siamo svegli e quando dormiamo.

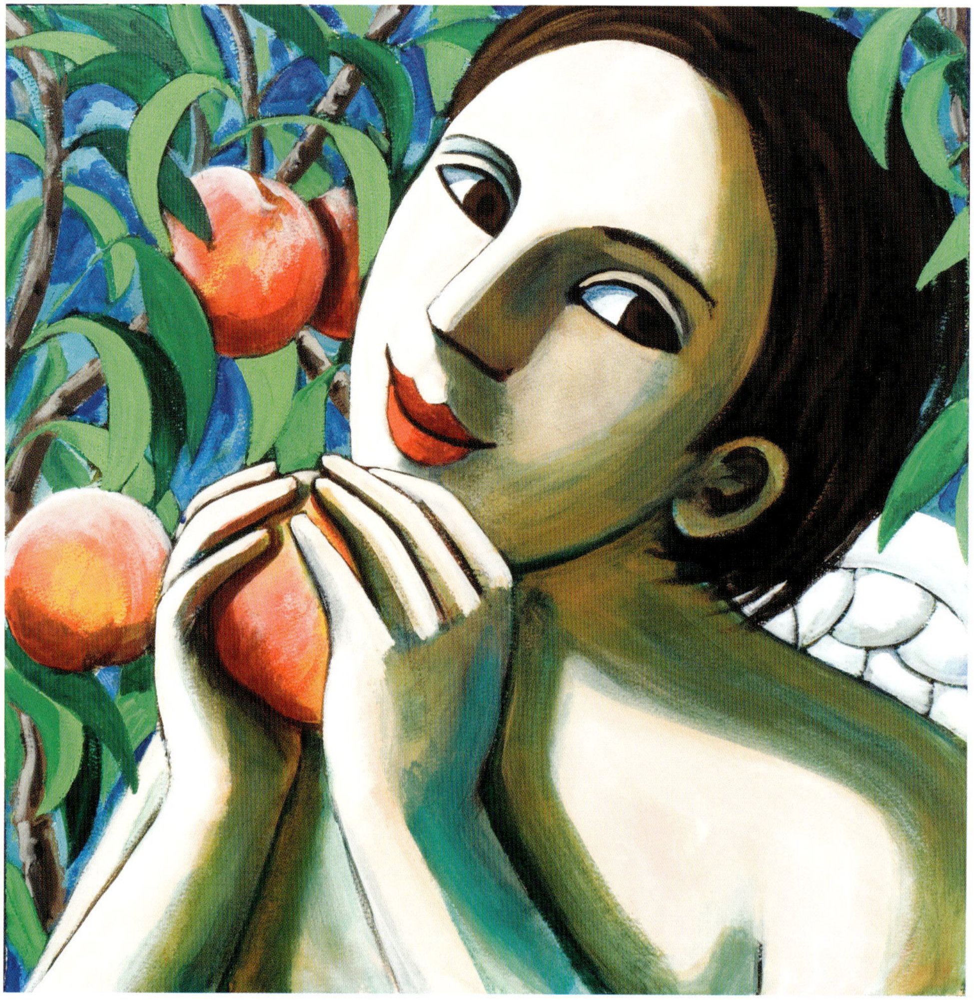

Angelo della Pesca

These things I warmly wish for you: Someone to love, some work to do, a bit o' sun, a bit o' cheer, and a guardian angel always near. *Irish blessing*

Ti auguro affettuosamente queste cose: qualcuno da amare, qualche lavoro da fare, un poco di sole, un poco di allegria e un angelo custode sempre vicino.

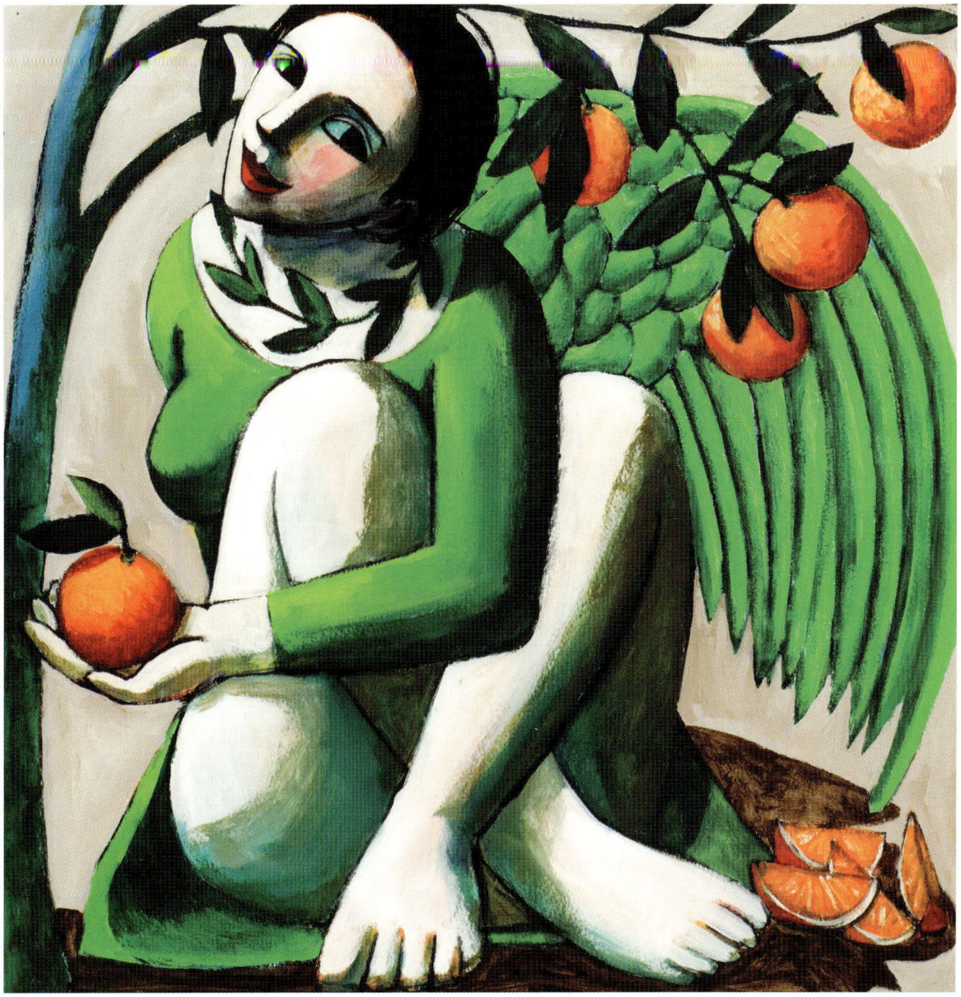

Angelo delle Arance

And as he lay and slept under a juniper tree, behold, then an angel touched him, and said unto him, Arise and eat. *Bible - Kings 19:5*

E dopo essersi sdraiato e addormentato sotto un ginepro, ecco che un angelo lo toccò e gli disse: “Alzati e mangia”.

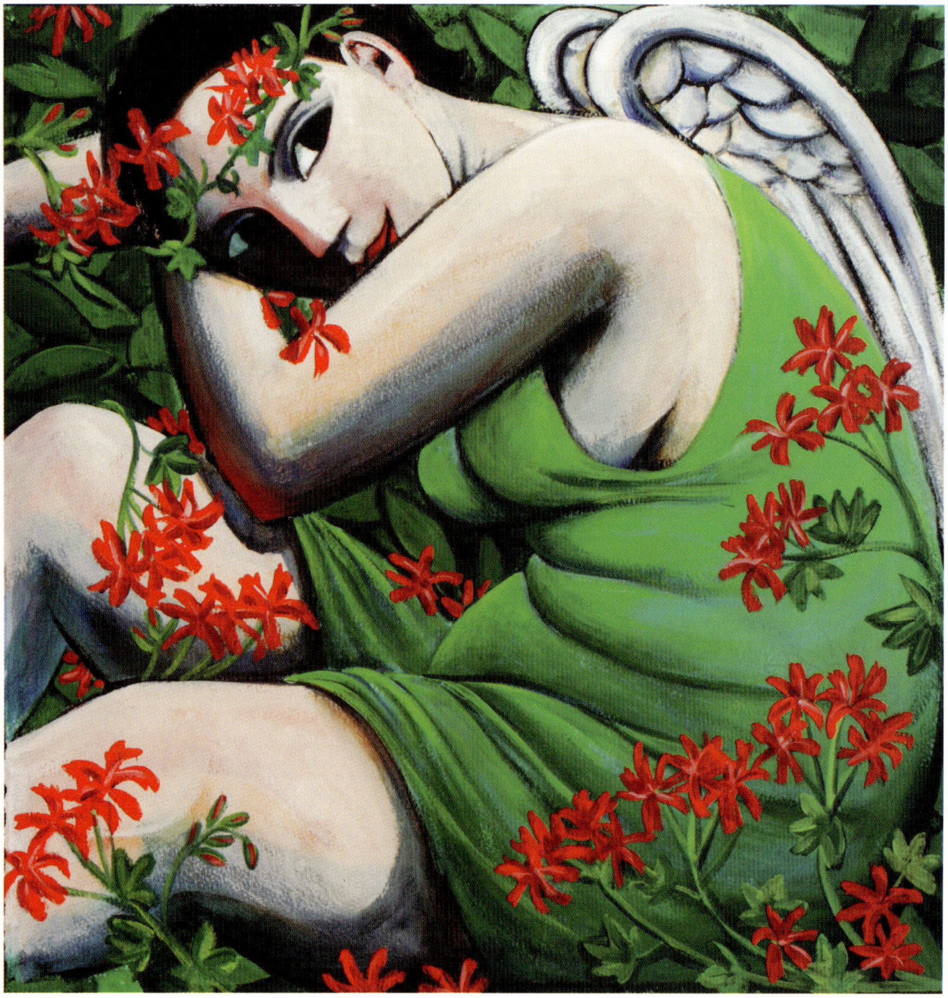

Angelo del Geranio

Have you ever seen a flower down
Sometimes angels skip around
And in their blissful state of glee
Bump into a daisy or sweet pea. *Jessi Lane Adams*

Hai mai visto un fiore piegato?
Qualche volta gli angeli saltellano in giro
E nel loro stato di gioiosa ebbrezza
Vanno a sbattere contro una margheritina o un pisello profumato.

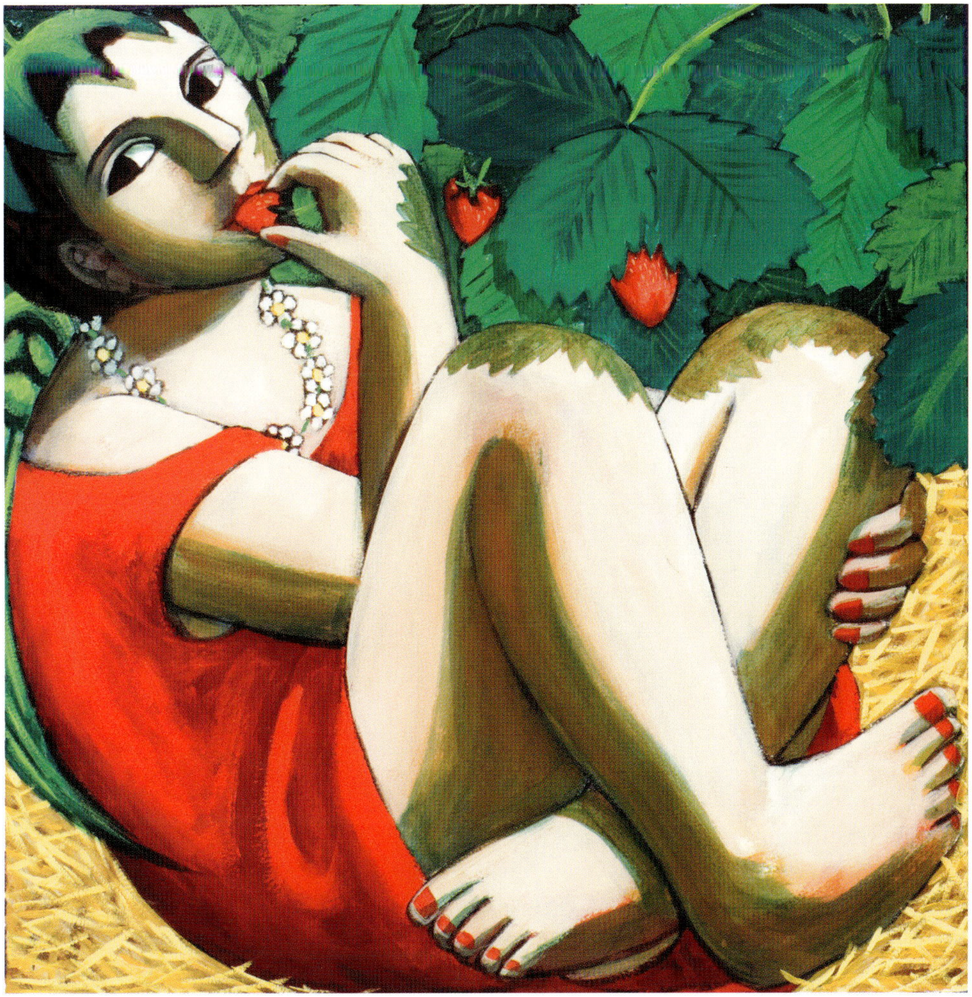

Angelo delle Fragole

We should not forget to entertain strangers, lest we entertain angels unaware. *Bible - Hebrews 13:2*

Non dovremmo mai dimenticare di dar ospitalità agli estranei, nel caso che, a nostra insaputa, questi siano angeli.

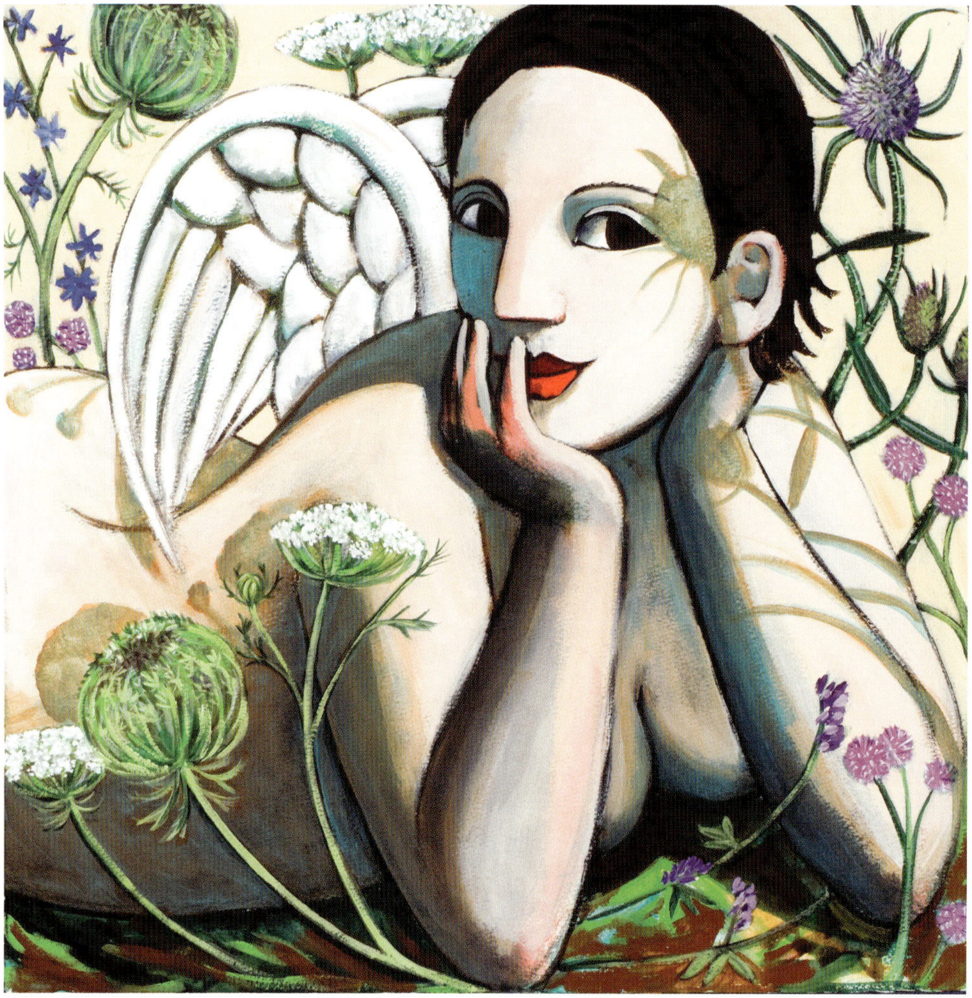

Angelo delle Erbacce

Flowers have spoken to me more than I can tell in written words. They are the hieroglyphics of angels, loved by all men for the beauty of the character, though few can decipher even fragments of their meaning. *Lydia M. Child*

I fiori mi parlano più di quanto io possa dire nelle parole scritte. Essi sono la scrittura in geroglifico degli angeli, amati da tutti per la bellezza dei caratteri, nonostante pochi possano decifrare perfino i frammenti del loro significato.

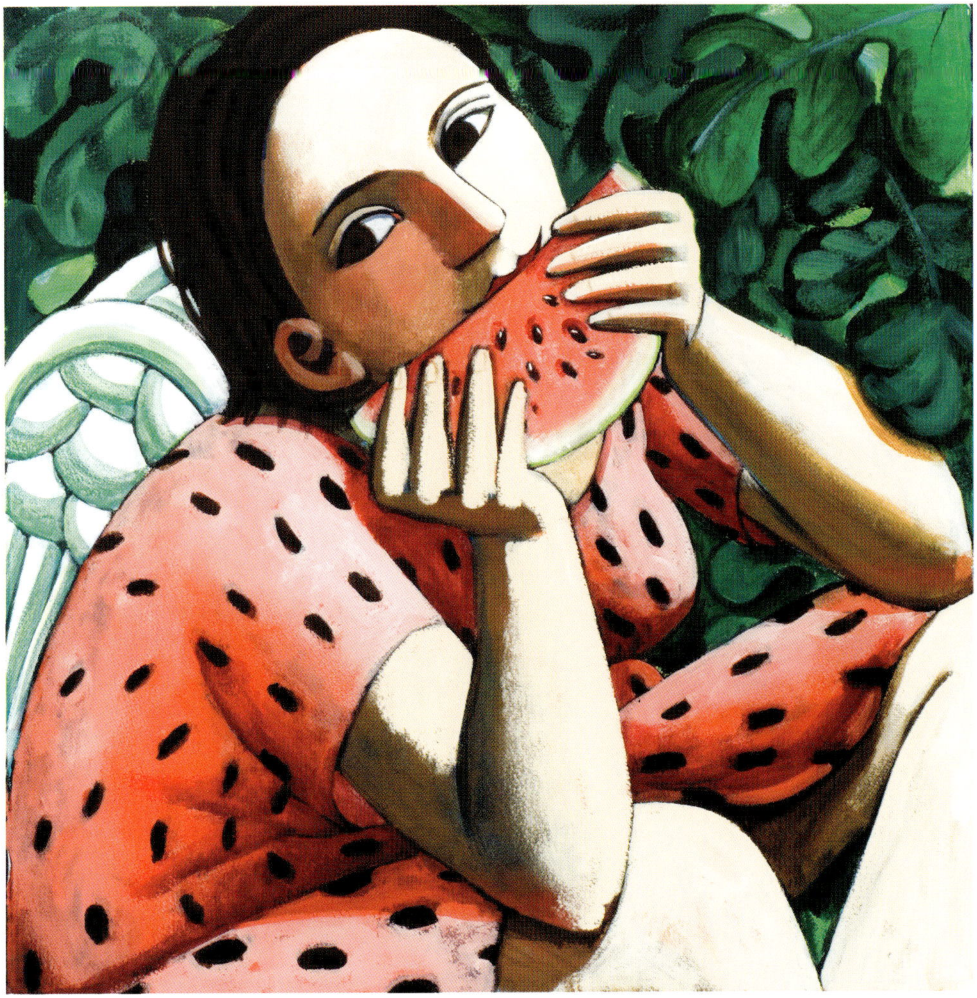

Angelo del Cocomero

When one has tasted watermelon he knows what the angels eat. *Mark Twain*

Quando si assaggia un cocomero si sa per certo che cosa mangiano gli angeli.

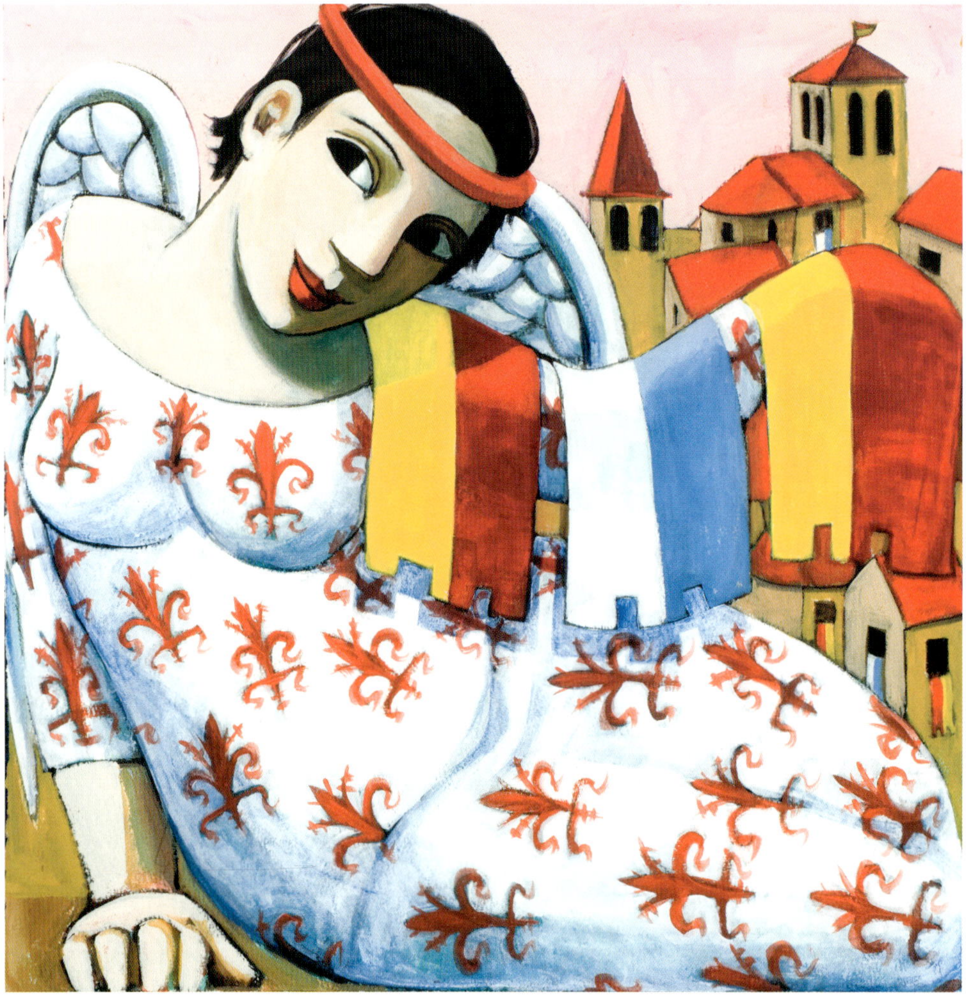

Angelo del Palio

We trust in plumed procession
For such the angels go -
Rank after Rank, with even feet -
And uniforms of Snow. *Emily Dickinson*

Confidiamo nel corteo piumato,
Perché così gli angeli marciano
In fila, con passo regolare
E le divise candide come la neve.

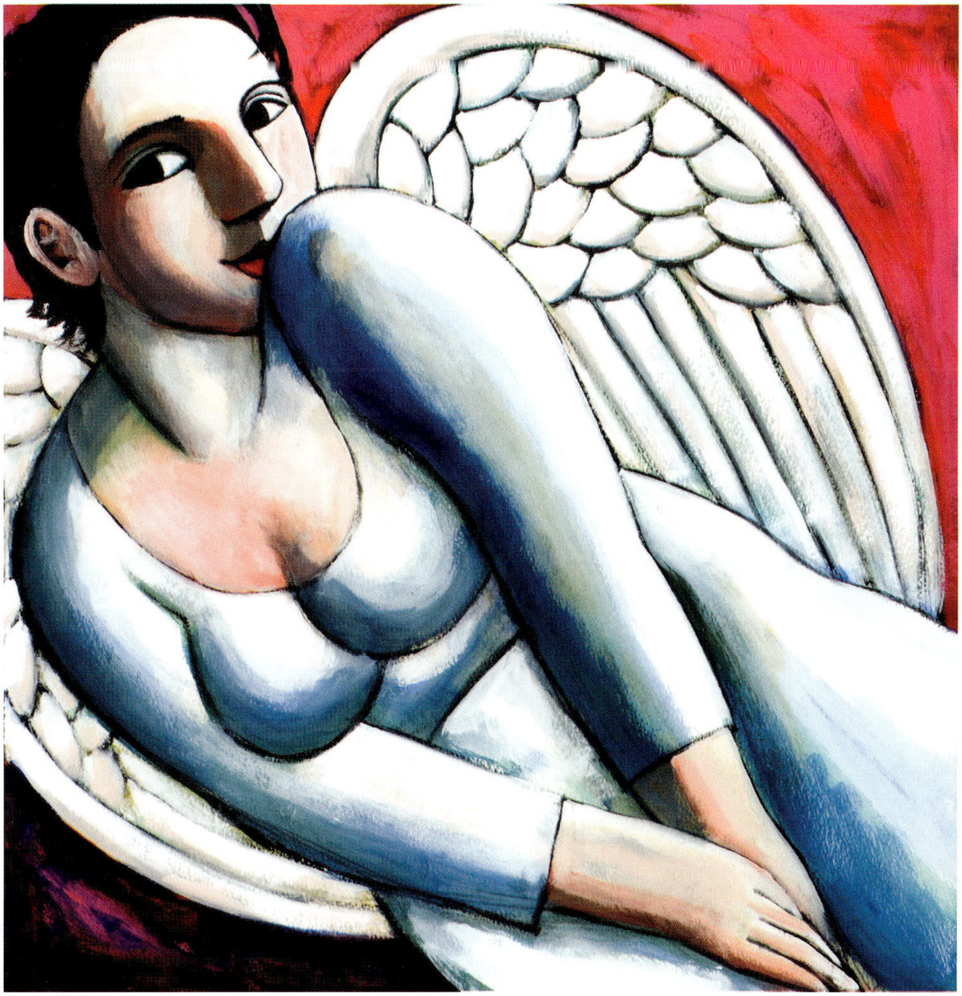

Angelo del Tramonto

My delight and thy delight
Walking, like two angels white,
In the gardens of the night. *Robert Bridges*

La mia gioia e la tua gioia
Che passeggiano, come due bianchi angeli
Nei giardini della notte.

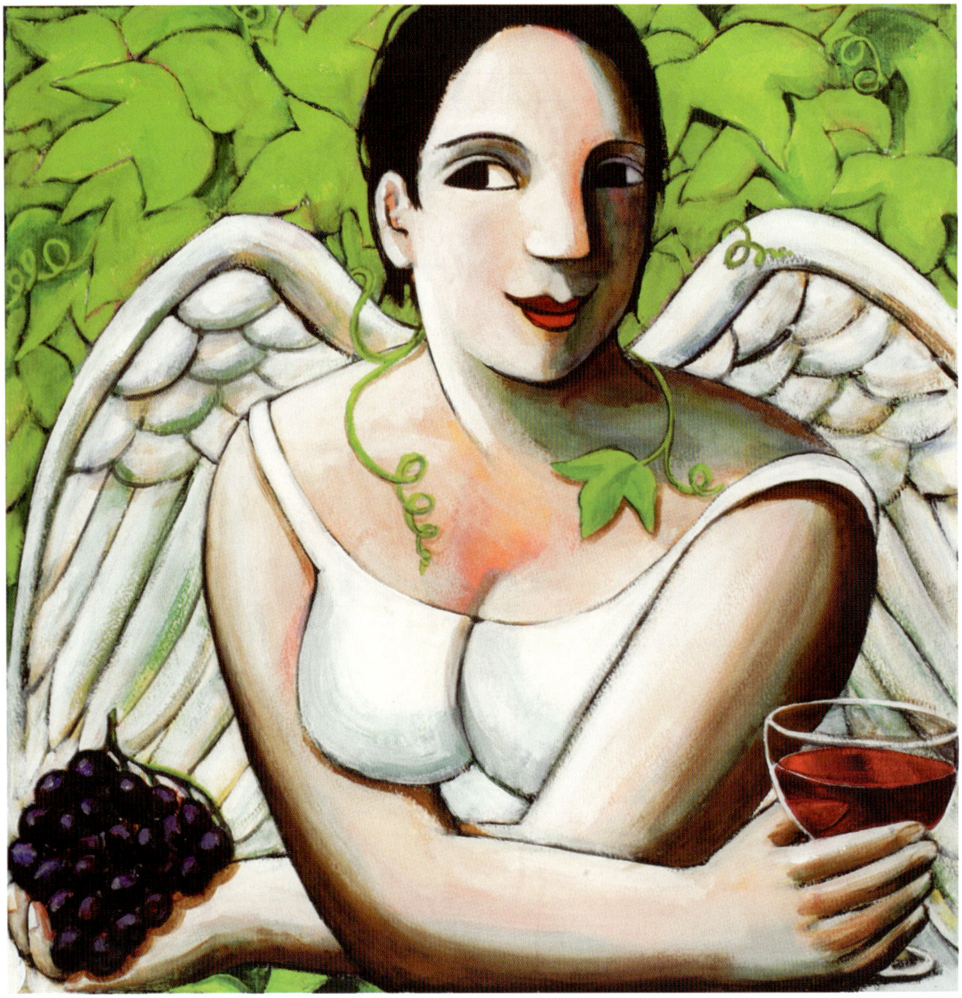

Angelo del Vino

Angels are speaking to all of us... some of us are only listening better.
Anonymous

Gli angeli parlano a tutti noi... però soltanto alcuni di noi sanno ascoltare.

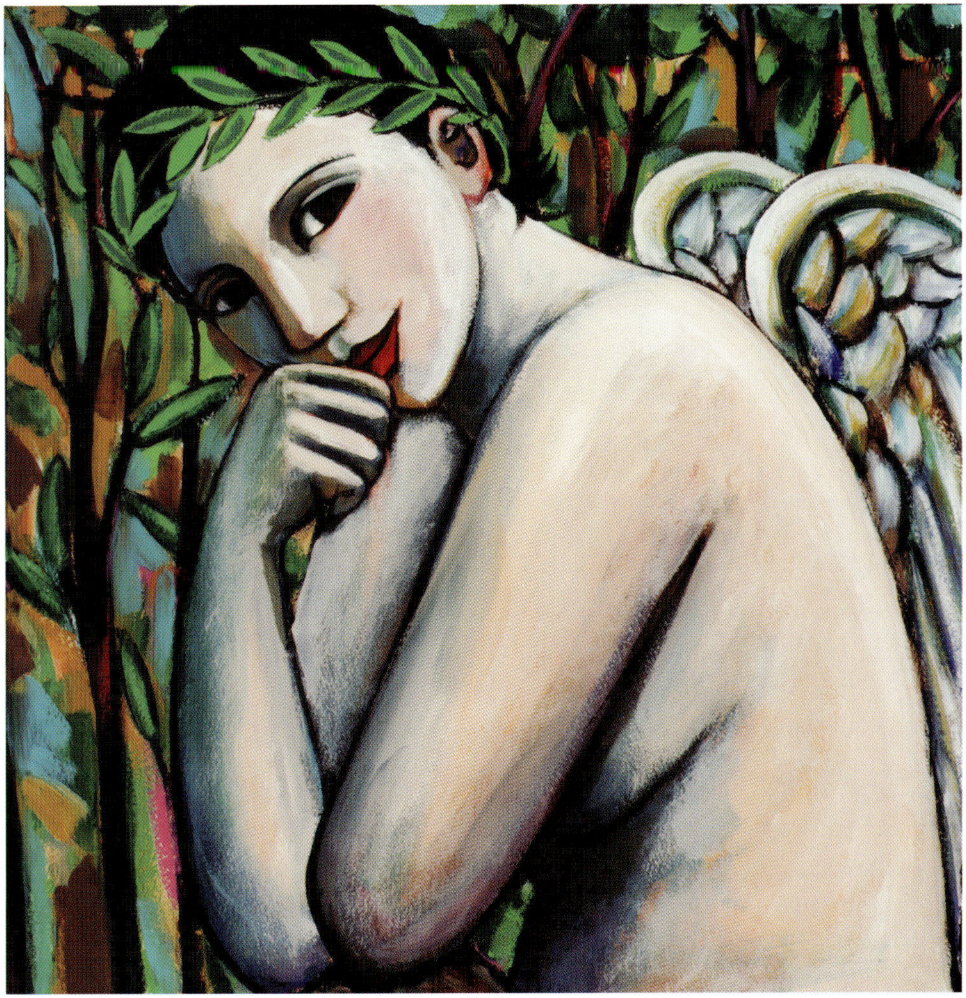

Angelo del Bosco

Ever felt an angel's breath in the gentle breeze? A teardrop in the falling rain? Hear a whisper amongst the rustle of leaves? Or been kissed by a lone snowflake? Nature is an angel's favorite hiding place. *Carrie Latet*

Hai mai sentito l'alito di un angelo nel venticello? Una lacrima nella pioggia che cade? Sentito un sussurro fra il fruscio delle foglie? O sei mai stato baciato da un fiocco solitario di neve? La natura è il nascondiglio favorito di un angelo.

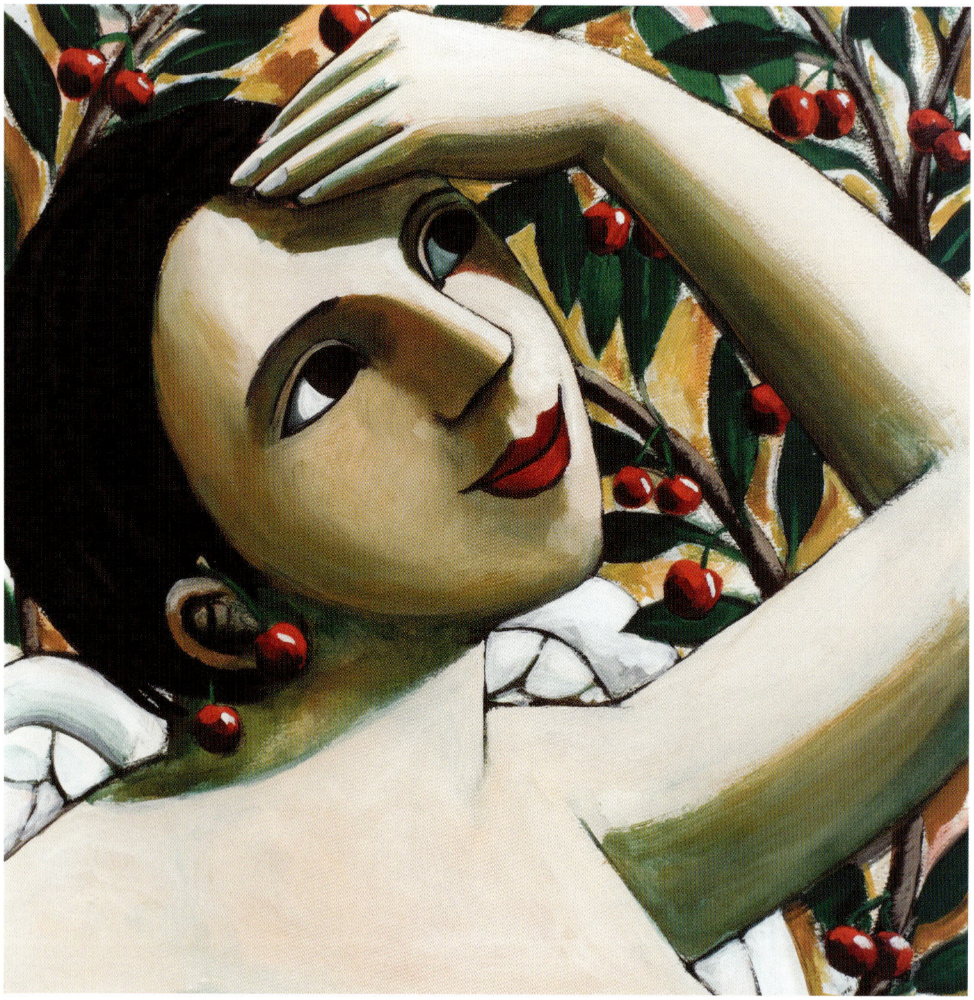

Angelo delle Ciliege

I went forth to find an angel
And found this effort brought
That life is full of so much good
The touch that angels wrought. *James Joseph Huesgen*

Sono andato a cercare un angelo
E questa faticosa ricerca mi ha insegnato
Che la vita è piena di grande bontà
È il tocco degli angeli.

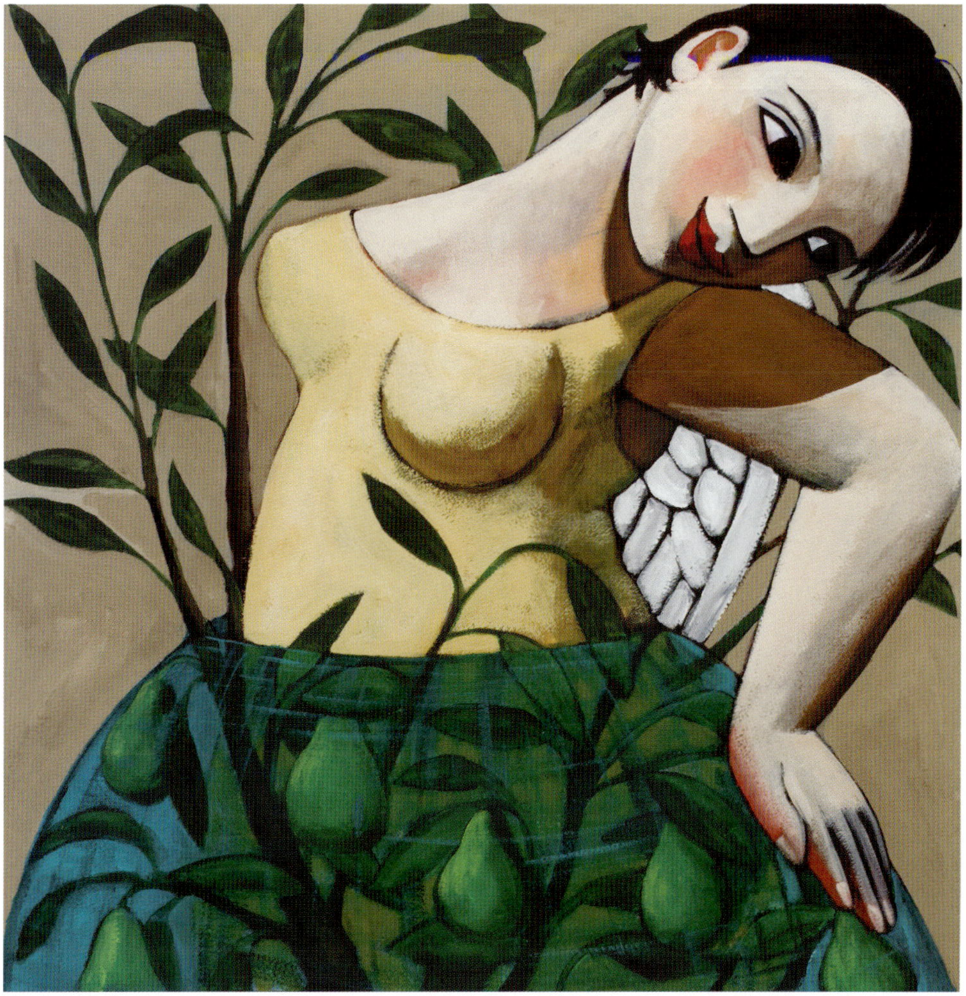

Angelo della Rete Antiuccelli

Angels are quite ample cause to cry... *Nicholas Gordon*

Gli Angeli sono una ragione più che sufficiente per piangere...

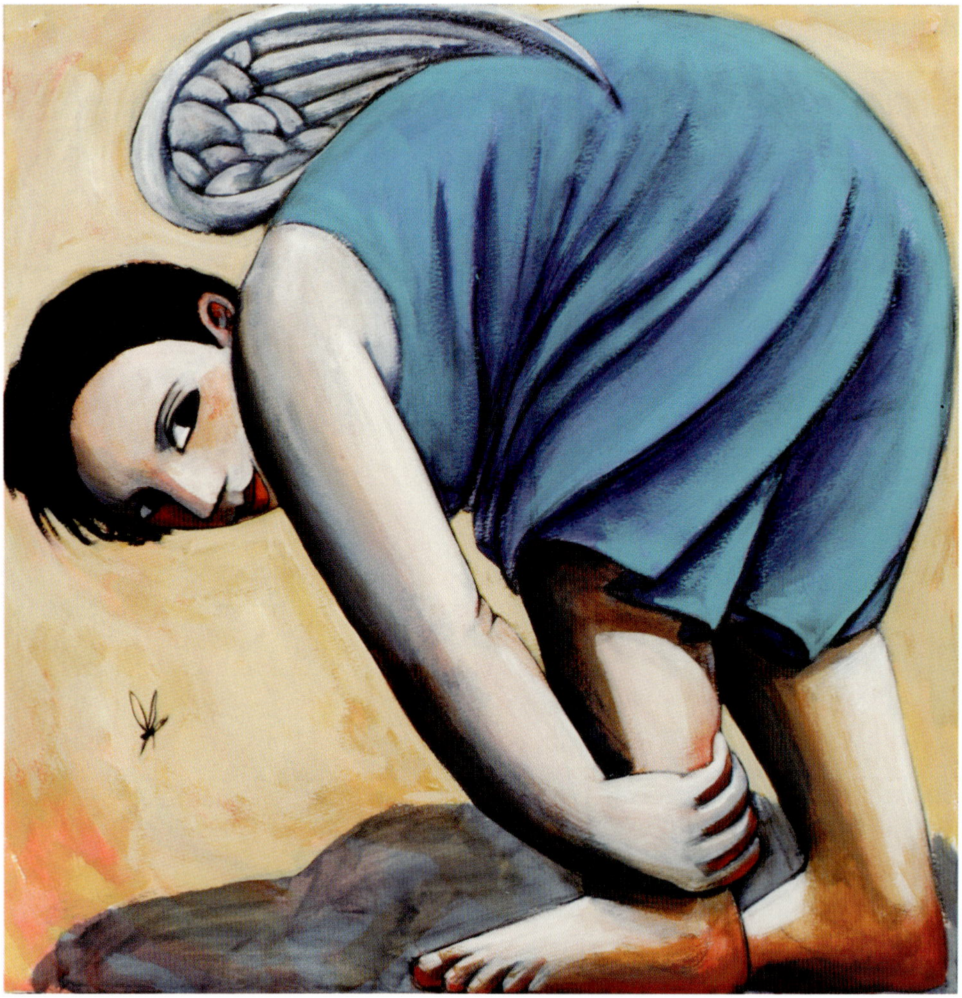

Angelo della Puntura di Zanzara

In Heaven an angel is nobody in particular. *George Bernard Shaw*

In paradiso un angelo non è nessuno di speciale.

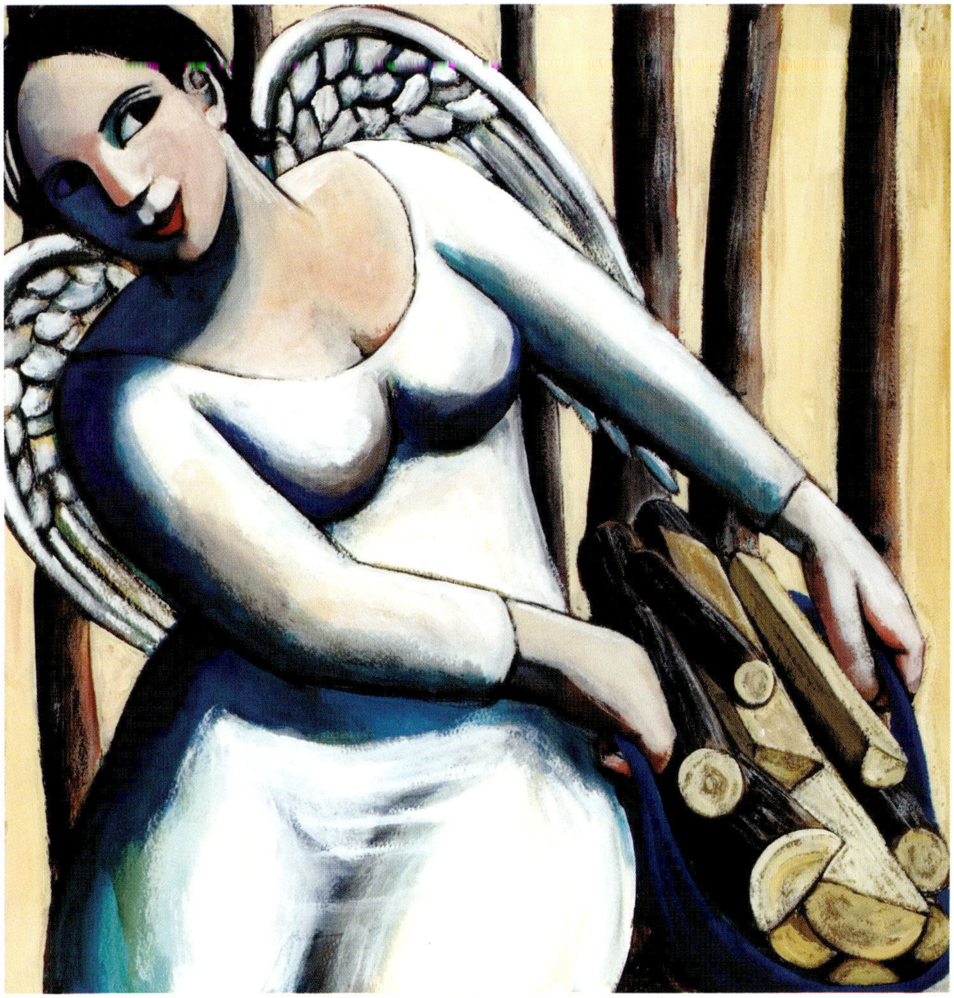

Angelo della Legna

You'll meet more angels on a winding path than on a straight one.
Daisey Verlaef

Incontrerai più angeli su una via tortuosa che su una strada dritta.

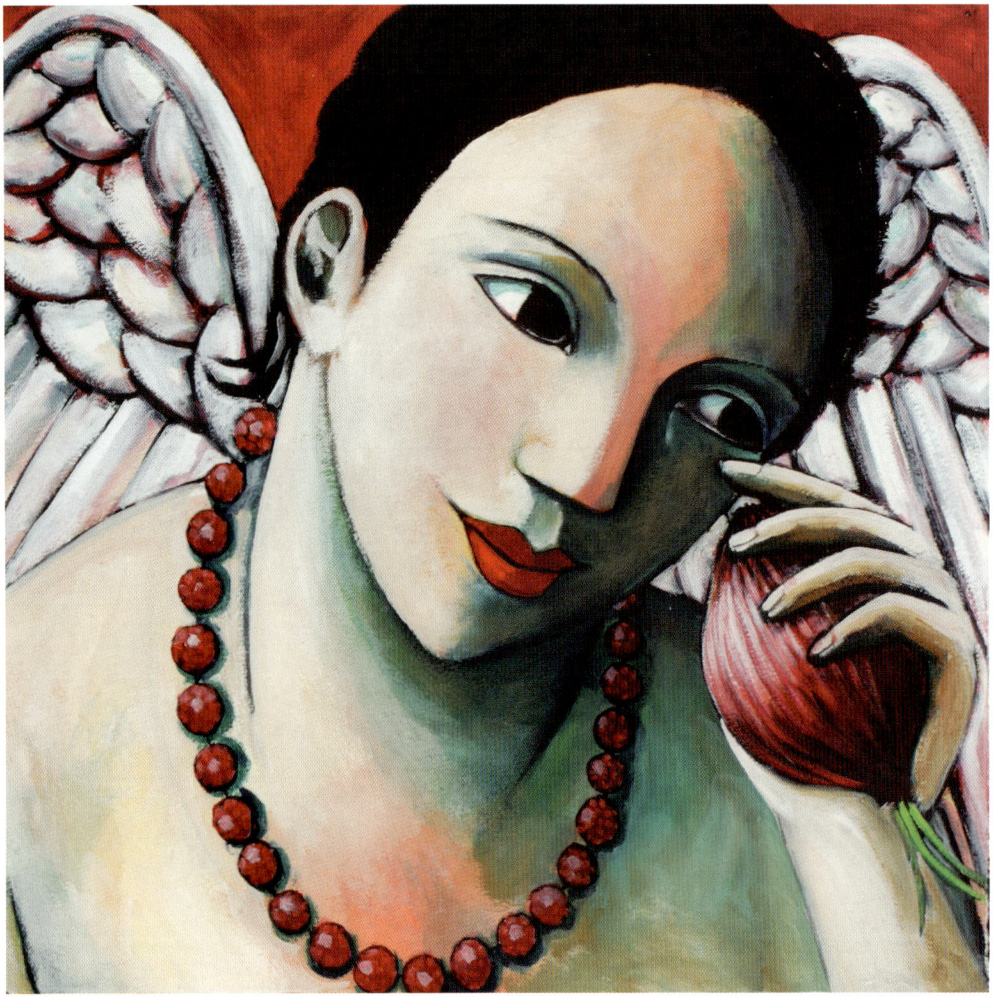

Angelo della Cipolla

May we live in peace without weeping. May our joy outline the lives we touch without ceasing. And may our love fill the world, angel wings tenderly beating.
Irish blessing

Che ci sia possibile vivere in pace senza piangere. Che la nostra gioia si trasmetta alle vite che tocchiamo, senza interruzione. E che il nostro amore riempia il mondo mentre le ali degli angeli pulsano morbidamente.

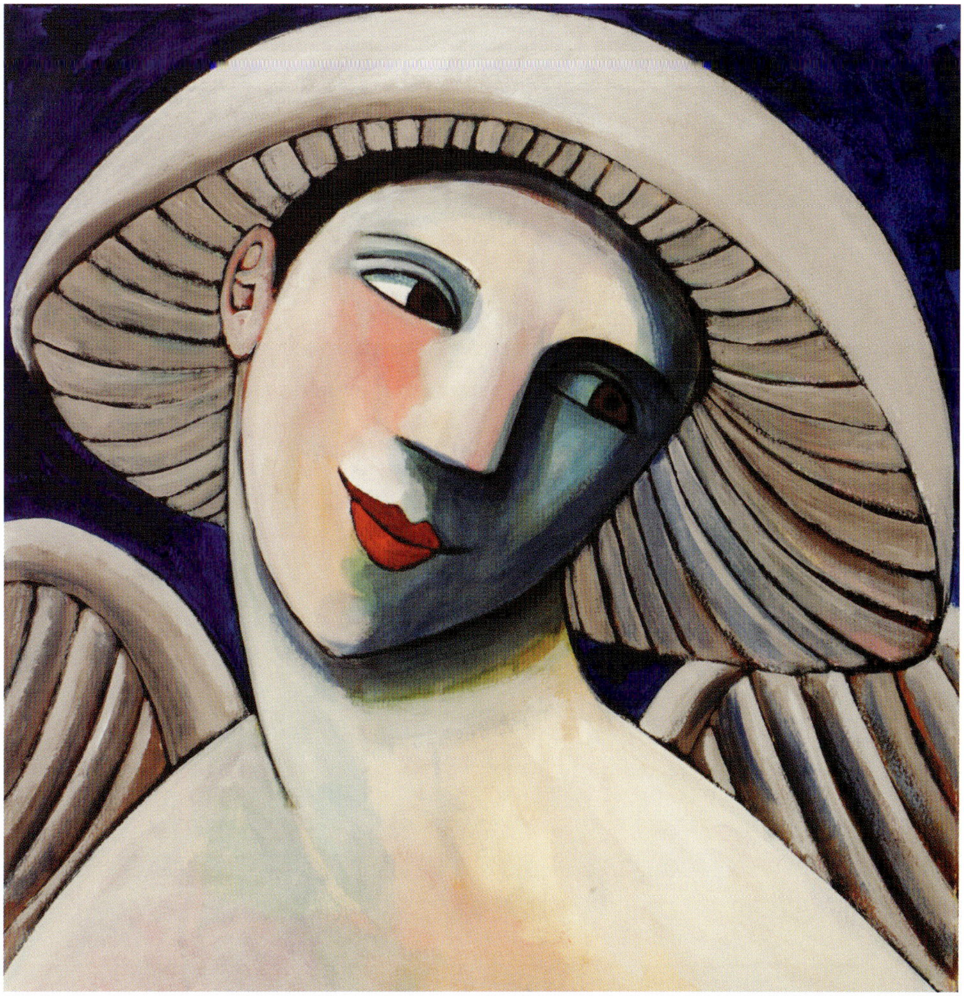

Angelo dei Funghi

The angels keep their ancient places;
Turn but a stone, and start a wing!
It's you, it's your estranged faces,
That miss the many-splendored thing. *Francis Thompson*

Gli angeli mantengono le loro antiche sedi
Alza una pietra e ci sarà un battito d'ala
Siete voi, sono i vostri volti alieni
Che non vedono tanto splendore.

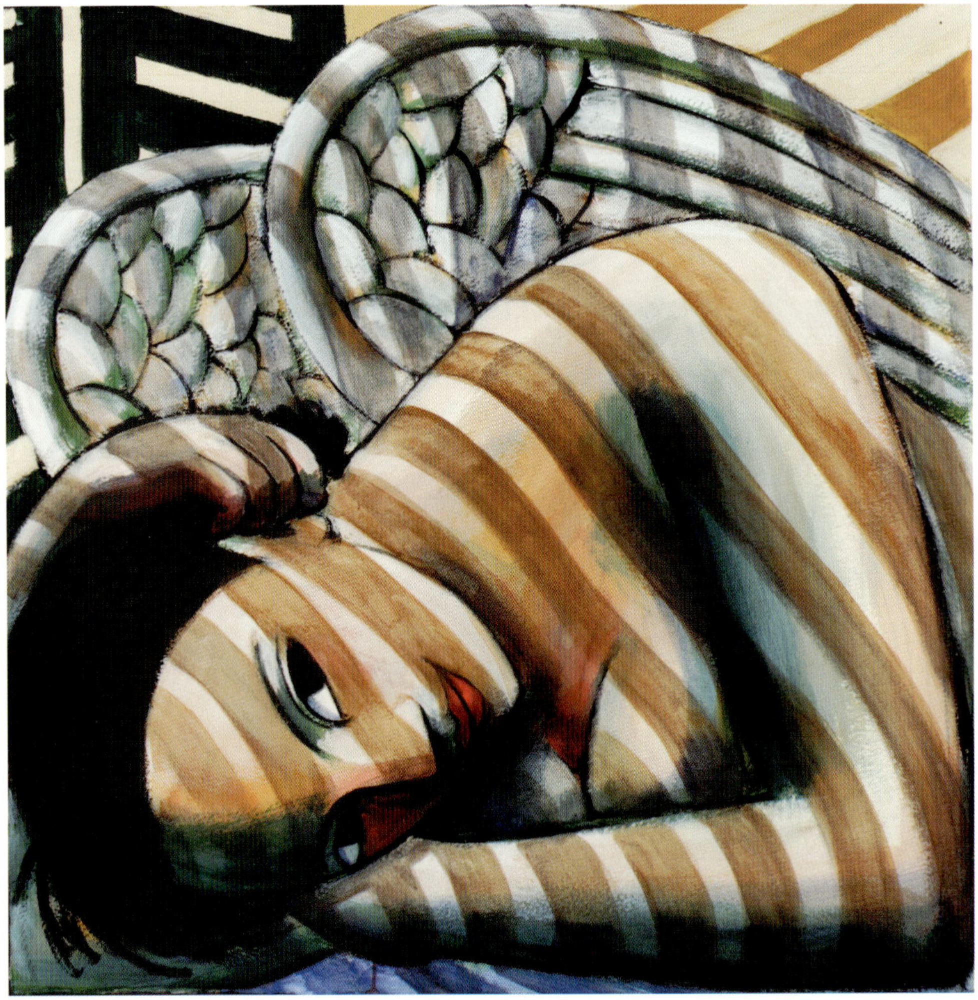

Angelo della Siesta

While we are sleeping, angels have conversations with our souls.
Anonymous

Quando dormiamo, gli angeli conversano con le nostre anime.

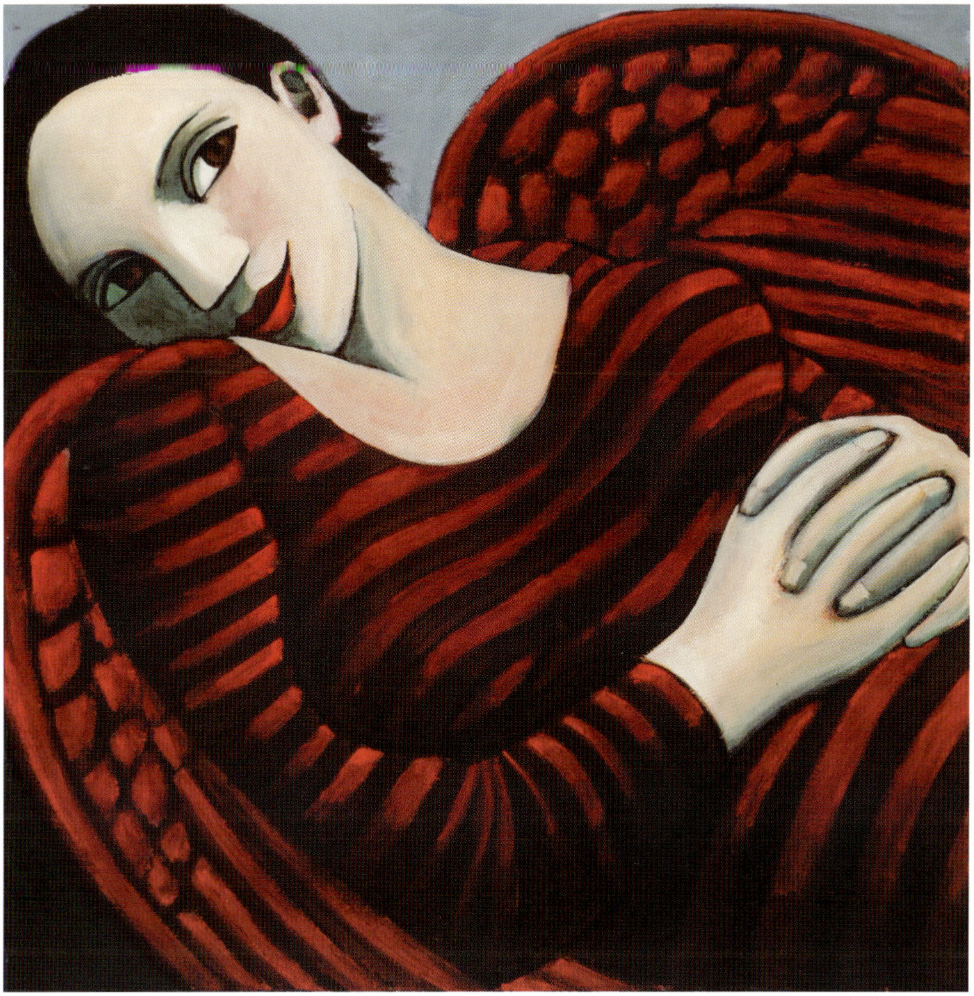

Angelo del Campo Arato

I'm no angel, but I've spread my wings a bit. *Mae West*

Non sono un angelo, ma ho aperto le mie ali un poco.

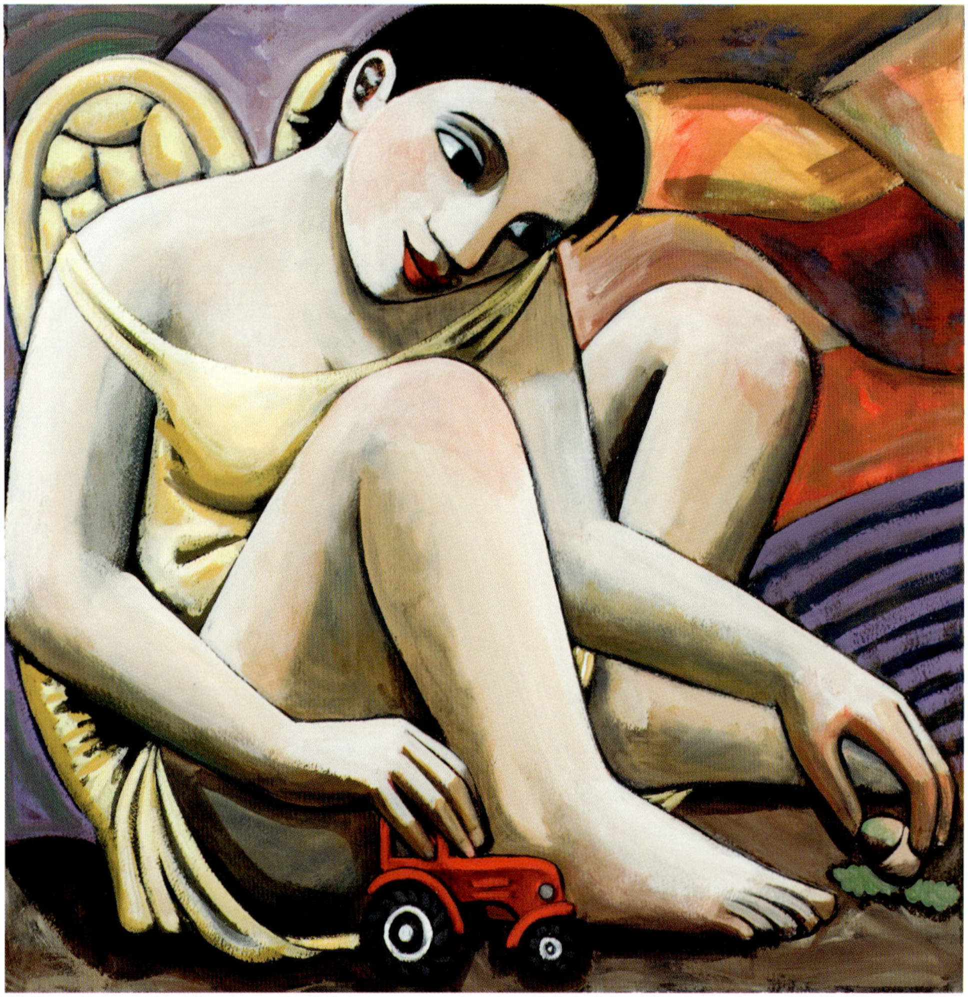

Angelo della Ghianda

The greatest achievement was at first and for a time a dream. The oak sleeps in the acorn, the bird waits in the egg, and in the highest vision of the soul a waking angel stirs. Dreams are the seedlings of realities. *James Allen*

La conquista più grande era all'inizio un sogno. La quercia dorme nella ghianda, l'uccello aspetta nell' uovo e un angelo si risveglia nella visione più alta dell'anima. I sogni sono i germogli della realtà.

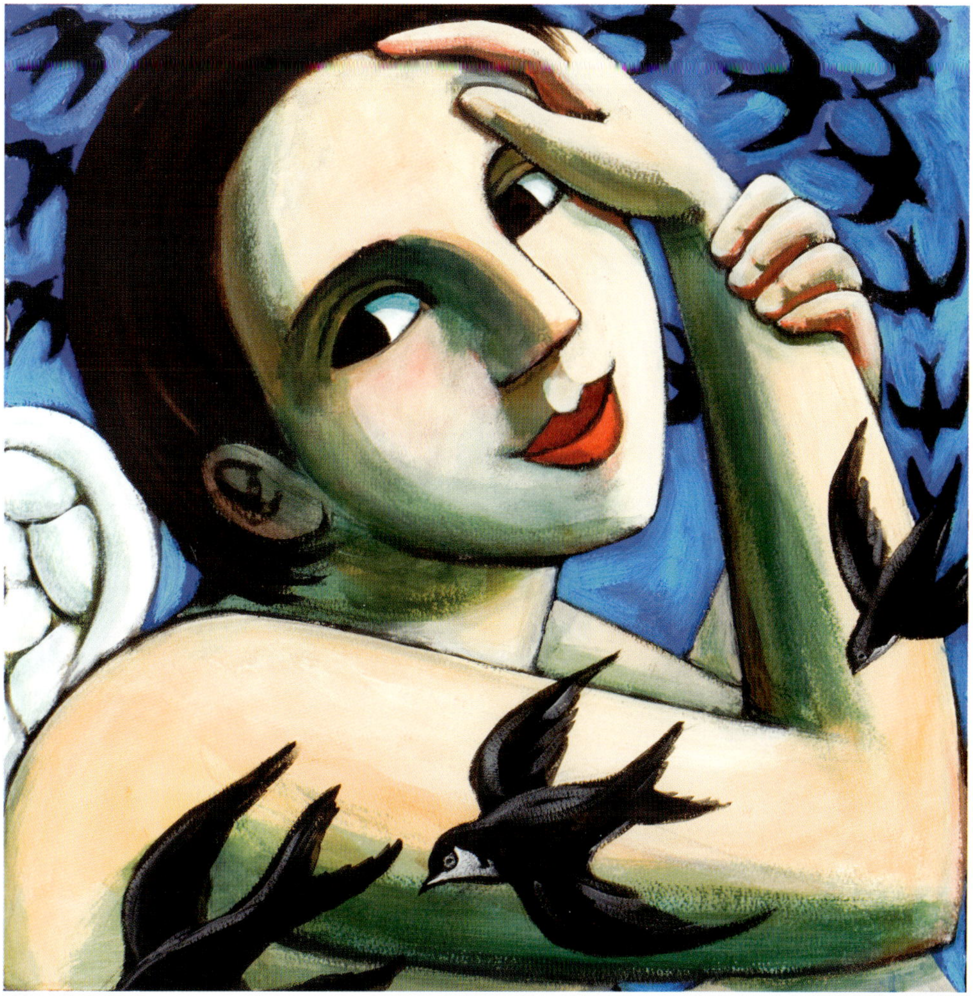

Angelo dei Rondoni

All God's angels come to us disguised. *James Russell Lowell*

Tutti gli angeli di Dio si presentano a noi mascherati.

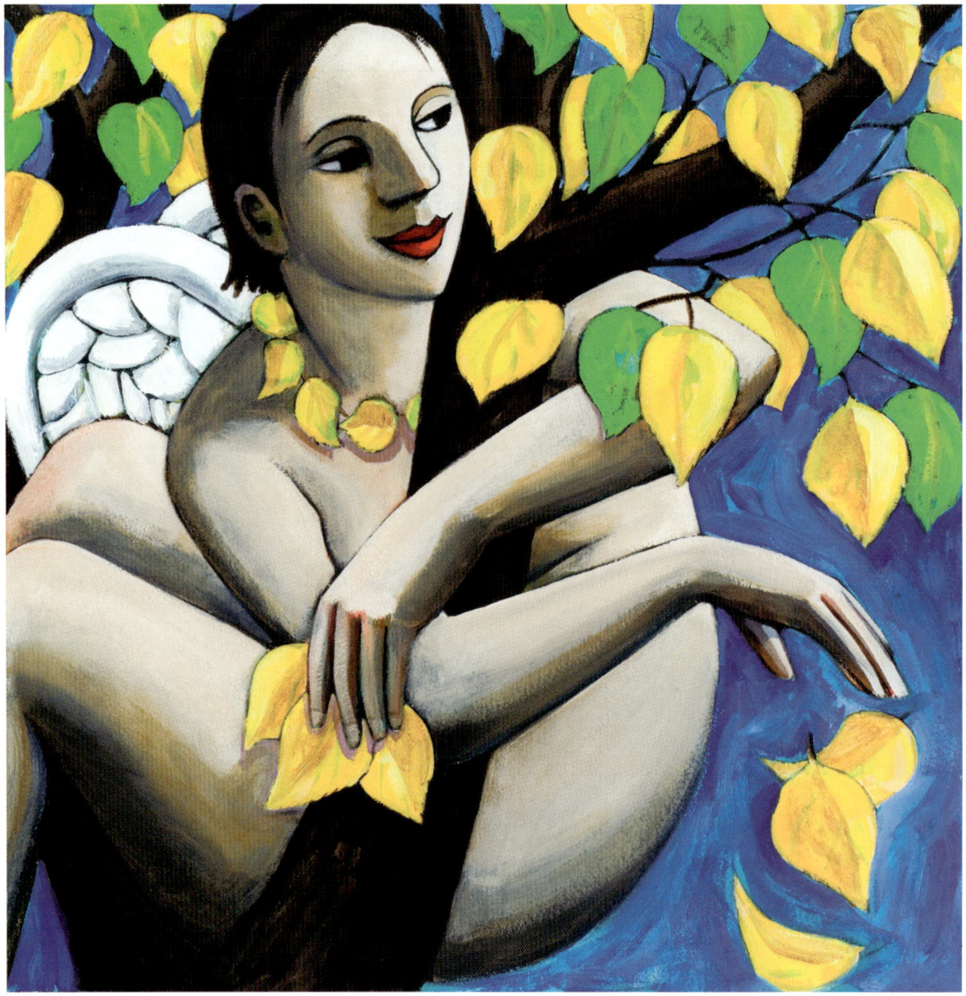

Angelo delle Foglie che Cadono

The Angels were all singing out of tune
And hoarse with having little else to do
Excepting to wind up the sun and moon
Or curb a runaway young star or two. *George Gordon, Lord Byron*

Gli angeli cantavano rauchi e stonati
Non avendo nient'altro da fare
Eccetto che infastidire il sole e la luna
O tenere a freno qualche giovane stella in fuga.

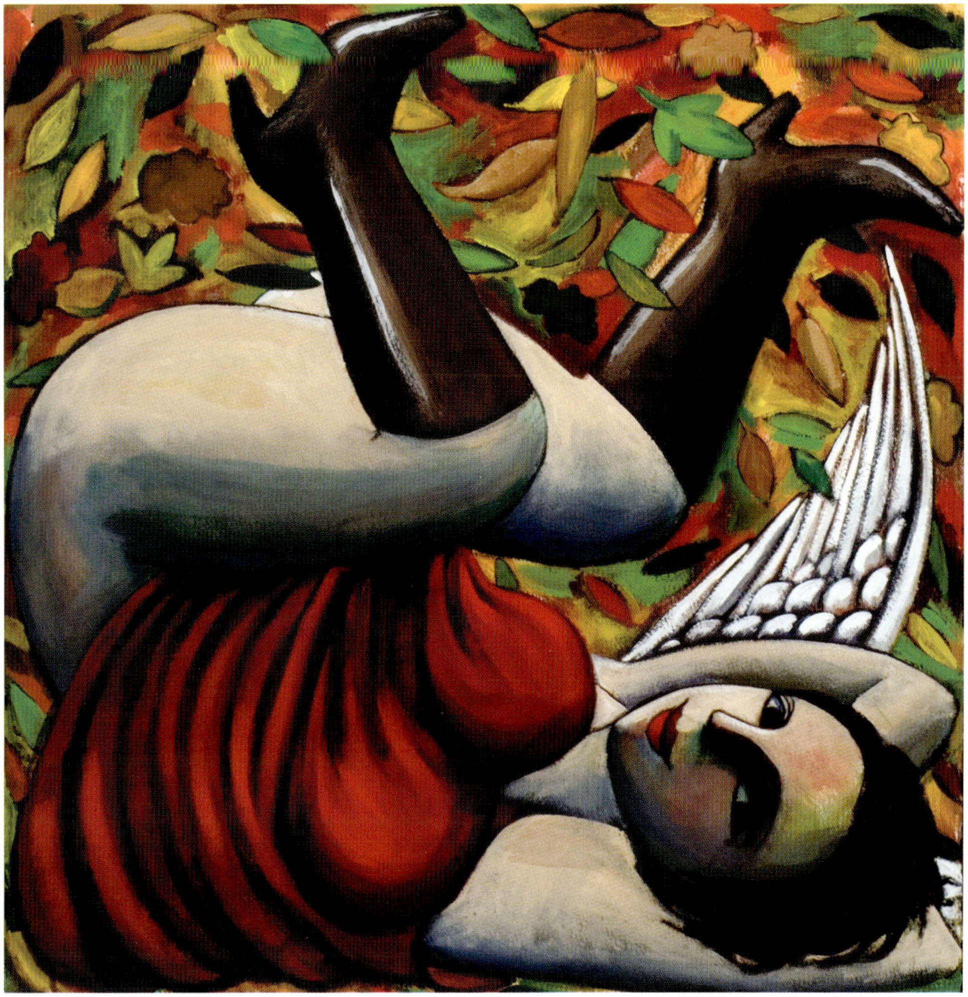

Angelo degli Stivali

There is joy in the presence of the angels. *Bible - Luke 15:10*

Quando ci sono degli angeli c'è sempre molta felicità.

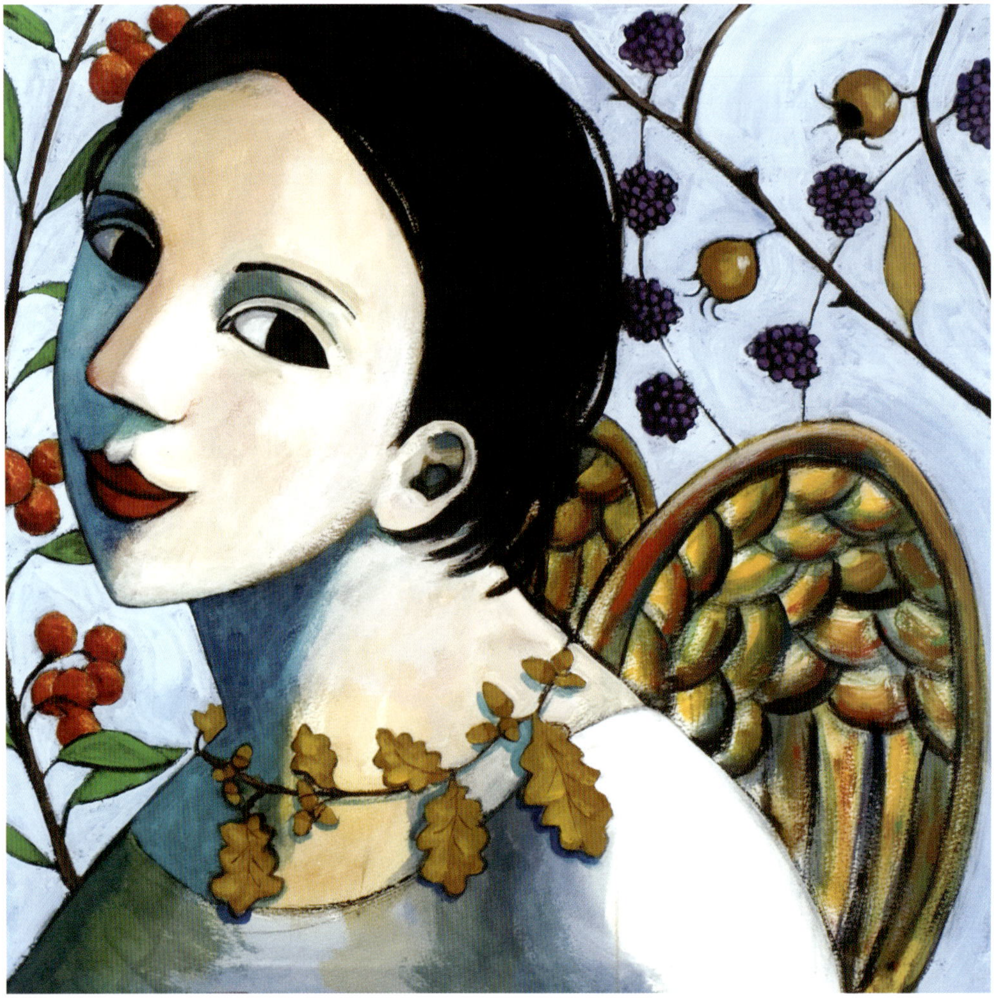

Angelo dell' Autunno

I saw angelic grace on Earth,
and heavenly beauty alone in the world. *Petrarch*

I' vidi in terra angelici costumi
e celesti bellezze al mondo sole.

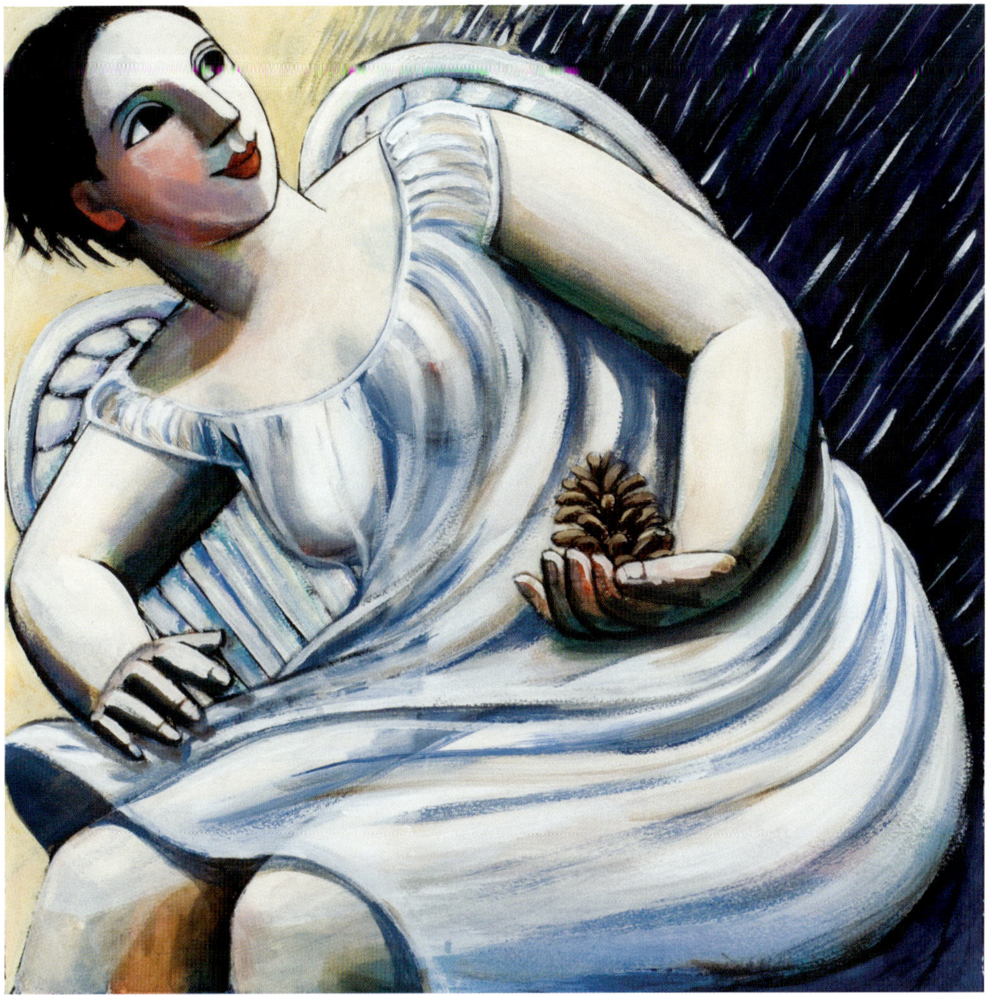

Angelo del Tempo che Cambia

Every breath of air and ray of light and heat, every beautiful prospect, is, as it were, the skirts of their garments.
(Referring to angels) John Henry Newman, Sermon - Michaelmas Day 1831

Ogni boccata d'aria, ogni barlume di luce, ogni soffio d'aria caldo, ogni bel panorama sono, per così dire, le gonne che loro indossano.

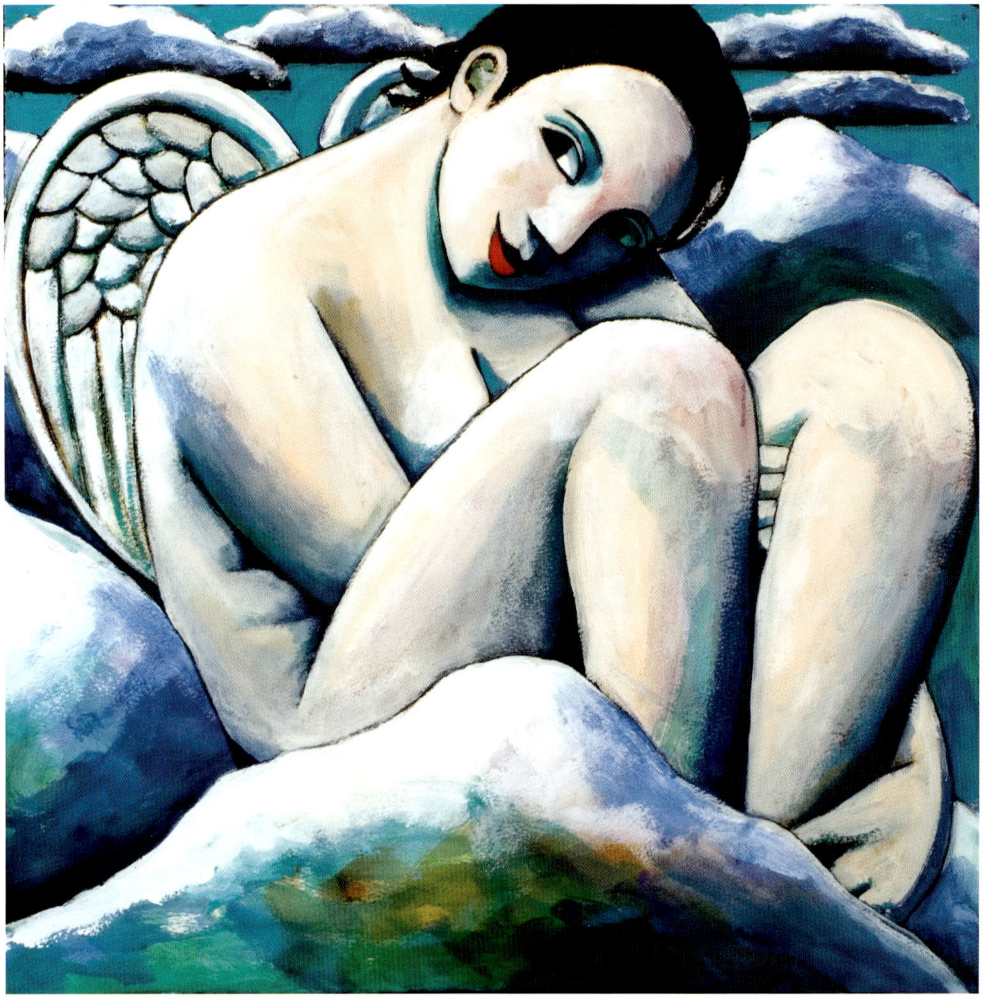

Angelo della Neve

There was a pause - just long enough for an angel to pass, flying slowly.
Ronald Firbank - Vainglory

Ci fu una pausa, della durata sufficiente per il passaggio di un angelo che volava lentamente.

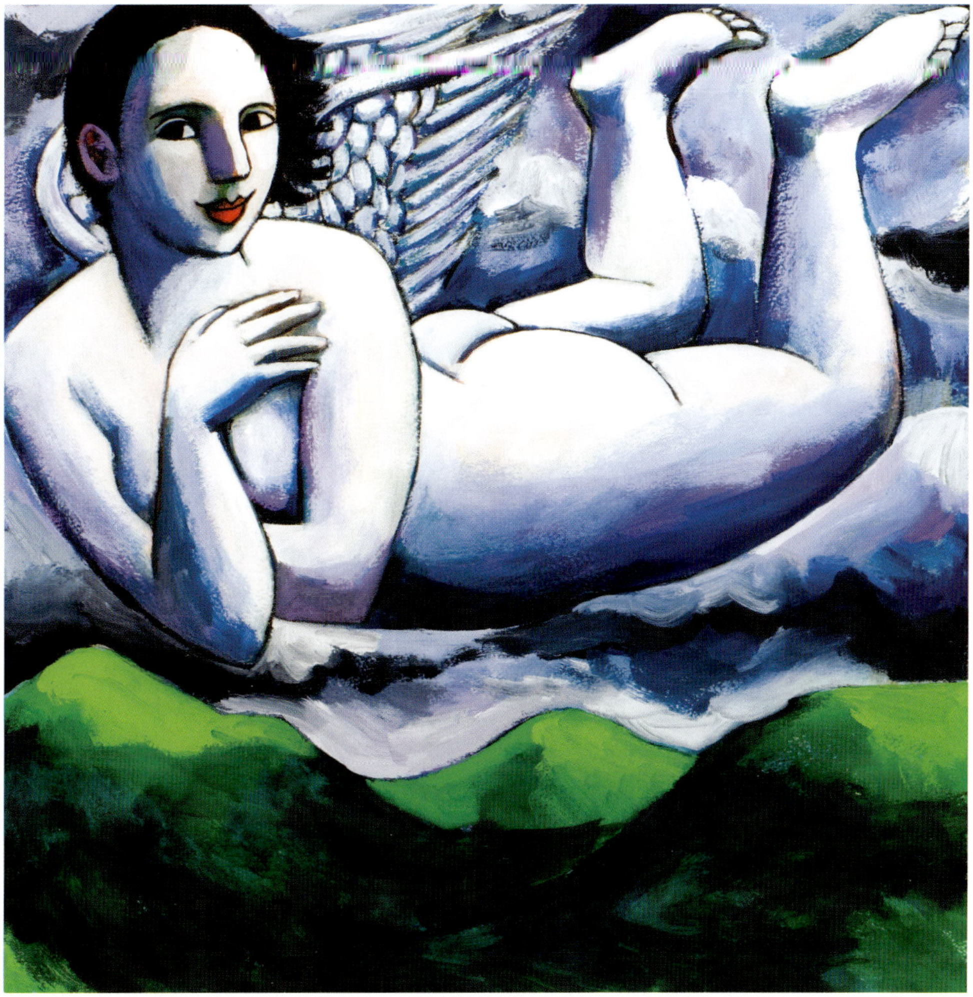

Angelo della Nuvola Nera

How wonderful it would be to see angels where there are only clouds.
How sad it would be to see only clouds where there are angels. *Anonymous*

Che splendido sarebbe vedere gli angeli dove ci sono solo nuvole. Che triste sarebbe invece vedere solo nuvole dove ci sono gli angeli.

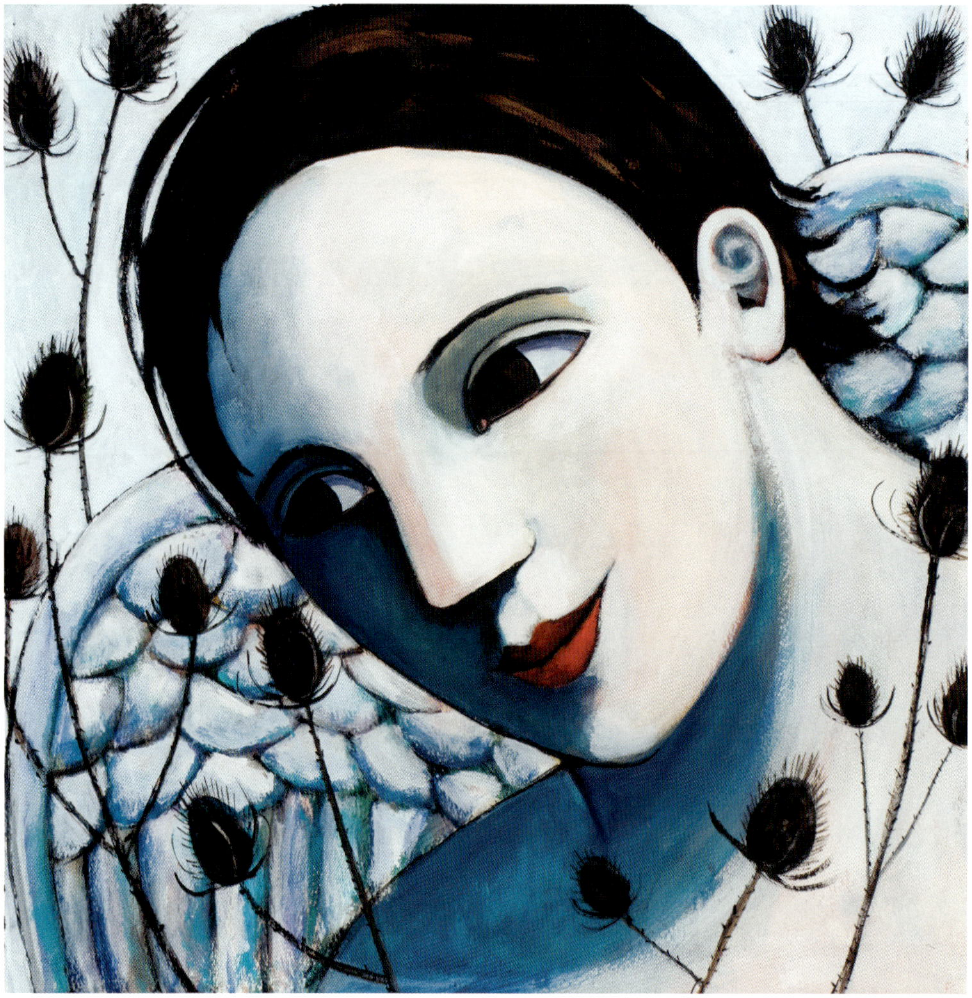

Angelo dell'Inverno

Thorns and stings
And those such things
Just make stronger
Our angel wings. *Emme Woodhull-Bäche*

Le spine e le asprezze
E quel genere di cose
Rendono più forti
Le nostre ali d'angelo

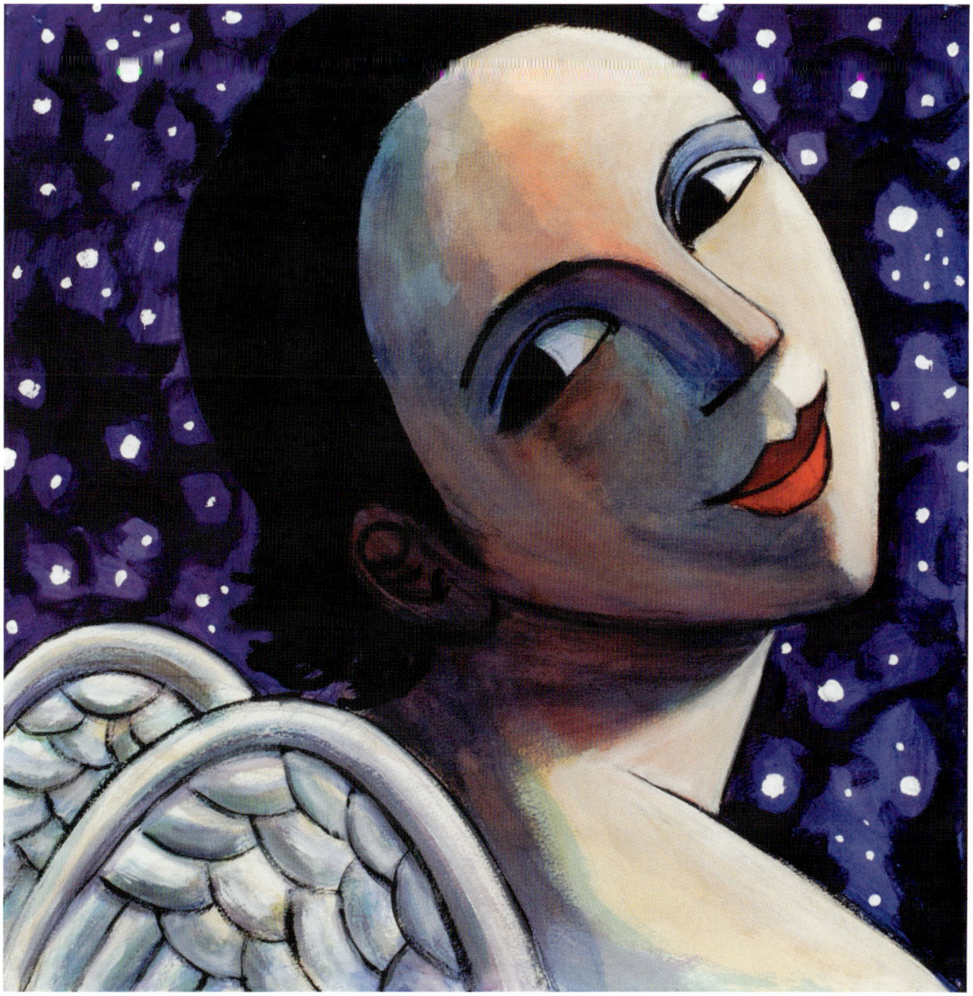

Angelo delle Stelle

We shall find peace. We shall hear the angels, we shall see the sky sparkling with diamonds. *Anton Chekhov*

Troveremo pace. Sentiremo gli angeli, vedremo il cielo scintillare pieno di diamanti.

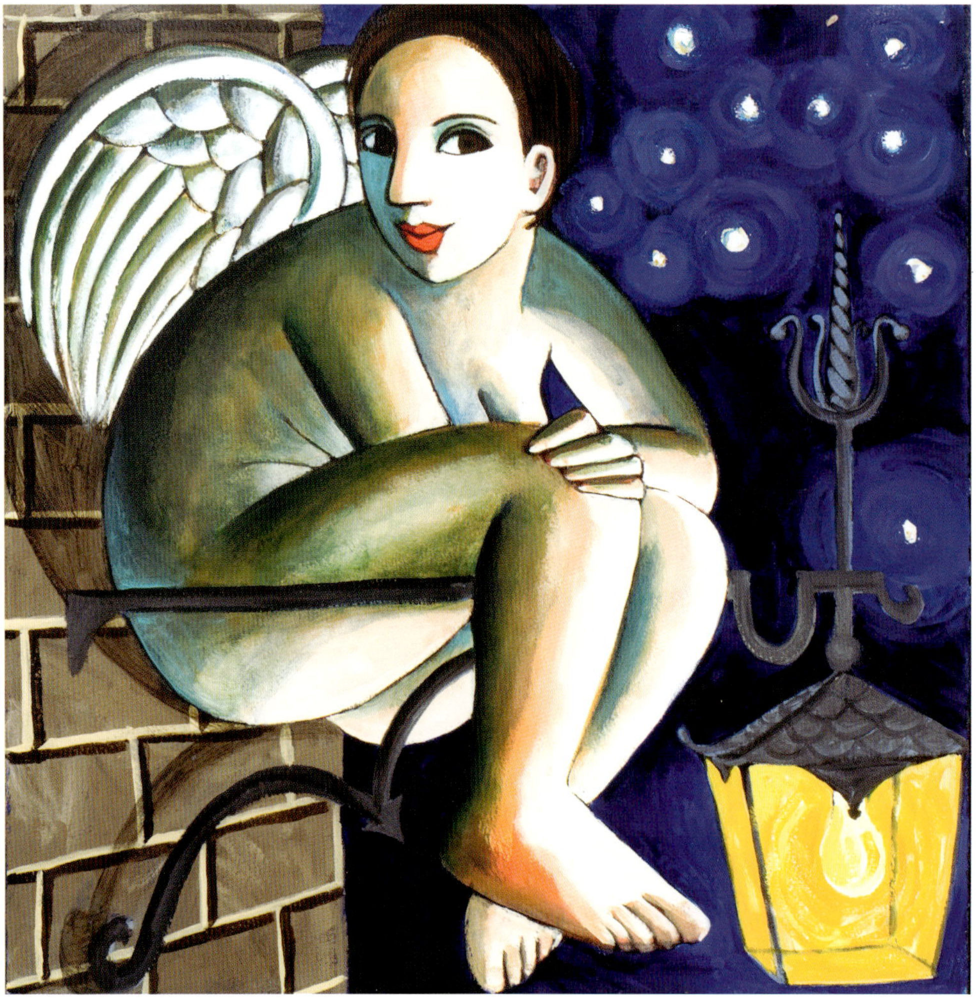

Angelo del Lampione

And so thy path shall be a track of light,
like angels' footsteps passing through the night.
Words on a church wall in Upwaltham England

E così il tuo cammino sarà una traccia di luce
Come le orme degli angeli che passano attraverso la notte.

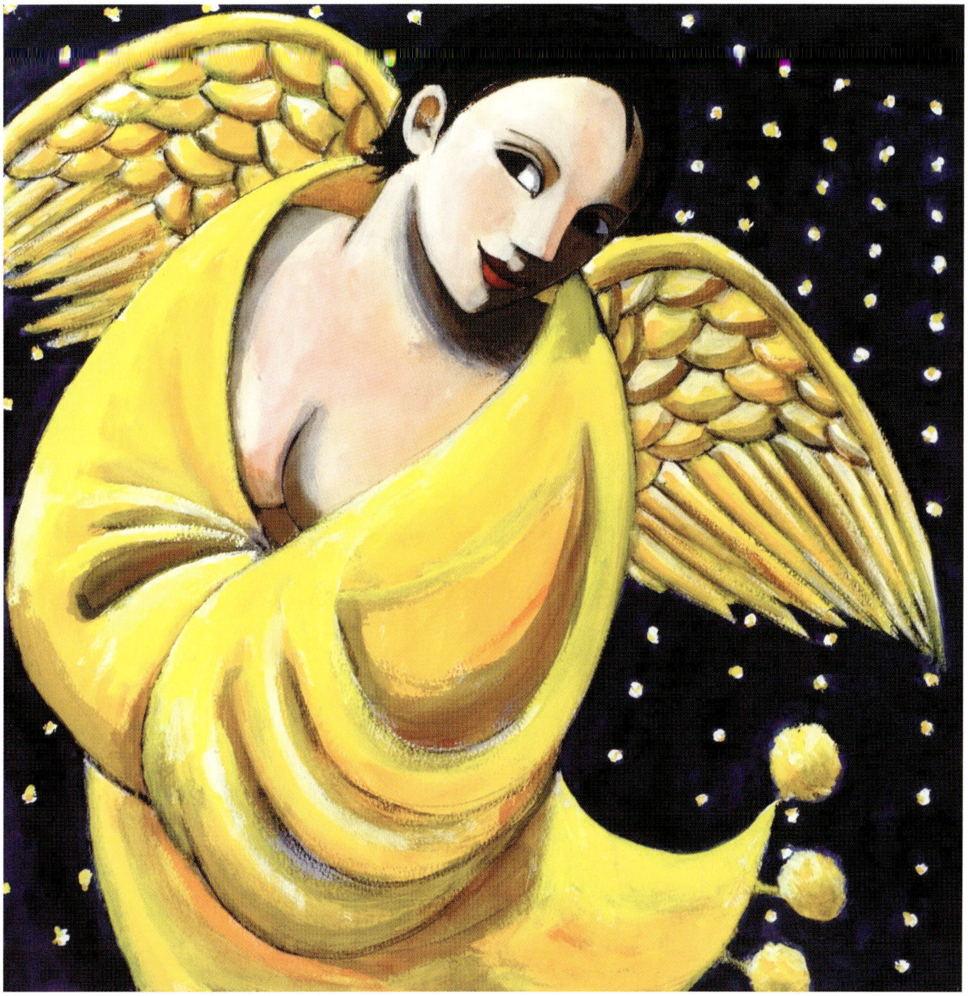

Angelo delle Luci di Natale

We are each of us angels with only one wing, and we can only fly by embracing one another. *Luciano de Crescenzo*

Gli uomini sono angeli con un'ala sola. Possono volare solo abbracciati.

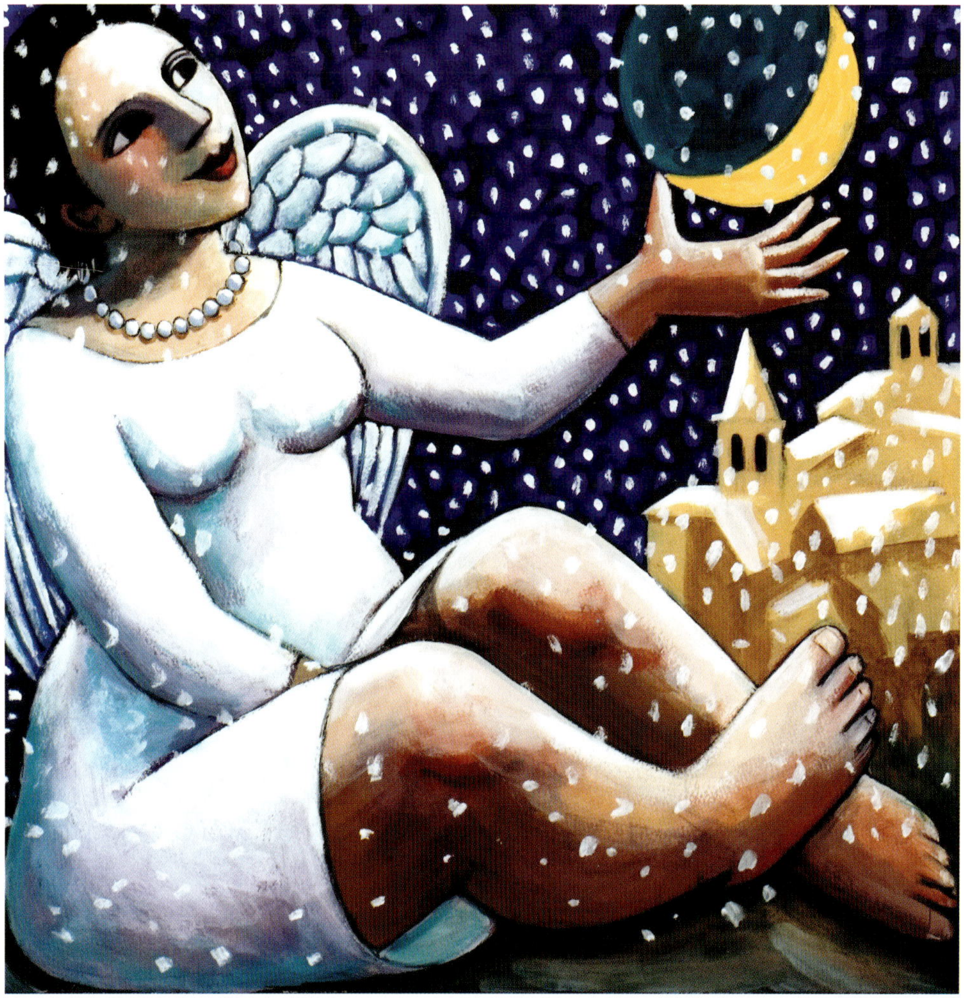

Angelo della Luna d'Inverno

The man, who has seen the rising moon break out of the clouds at midnight, has been present like an archangel at the creation of light and of the world.
Ralph Waldo Emerson

L'uomo che ha visto la luna alzarsi al di sopra delle nuvole a mezzanotte, è stato testimone, come un arcangelo, della creazione della luce e del mondo.